HUMANAE VITAE FORTY YEARS ON

A NEW COMMENTARY

G J WOODALL

FAMILY PUBLICATIONS • OXFORD

MARYVALE INSTITUTE

ISBN 978-1-871217-78-0

co-published by

Family Publications, Denis Riches House
66 Sandford Lane, Oxford OX1 5RP, UK
www.familypublications.co.uk

Centre for Marriage and Family at the Maryvale Institute
Maryvale House, Old Oscott Hill
Birmingham B44 9AG, UK
www.maryvale.ac.uk

Printed in England by
Cromwell Press, Trowbridge, Wilts.

CONTENTS

"If sexual intercourse becomes a drug and leads to subjecting one's partner to one's wishes and interests, without respecting the 'times' of the person loved, what has to be defended then is not only the true concept of love, but the dignity of the person as such ... "

"... No mechanical technique can substitute for the act of love which two spouses exchange as a sign of a greater mystery, which sees them as sharers in creation ... "

POPE BENEDICT XVI

10 May 2008, Allocution to Participants in a Congress at the
Lateran University, Rome (8-10 May 2008, to celebrate
the 40th anniversary of *Humanae vitae*)

FOREWORD

Why another translation of Paul VI's encyclical, the 40th anniversary of which we celebrate this year? The text of this controversial encyclical has been translated into English on a number of occasions. It seemed to me that to write a commentary on this text, paragraph by paragraph, a new examination of the official Latin text would be appropriate, indeed would be required. It has been my intention to avoid a very free translation, since it would be difficult to say that such was faithful to Paul VI's teaching, which has already been so disputed and misunderstood; a free translation would have added to the confusion. My aim has been to stay as close to the original wording as possible, to the extent that this was compatible with giving a clear understanding of the text and to the extent that it was compatible with the conventions of inclusive language.

For the purposes of clarity, long Latin sentences have been broken down at times and words have been added in brackets to show the continuing sense of the original; for example, "(It is asked)" in n. 3 § 1 and § 2, or "(This is so)" in n. 14 § 3 where n. refers to the numbered paragraphs of the encyclical and § to the sub-paragraphs within those numbered paragraphs.

In some other passages I have put the literal translation of a Latin word or phrase in brackets where a less literal expression was needed in the text to avoid stultified English (e.g. "authentic (right) love" and "acting in this way (doing these things)" in n. 16 § 3, lines 28-30). On two occasions I have given in brackets a technical word, which is used in the Latin and which has broader theological significance ("for sound (probable) reasons" in n. 16 § 3, line 16 and "obedience (obsequium)" in n. 28 line 12).

Good arguments have been put forward in the past for translating the word *'munus'* as 'mission': that this translation fits in with the translation of the term as it appears many times in the texts of the Second Vatican Council, that it evokes the participation of married couples in the mission of Christ and of the Church, etc.[1] It seems to me that this term is very well translated as 'mission' in many of those Conciliar texts and in *The Code of Canon Law* of 1983 in addressing the functions of Jesus Christ as priest, prophet and shepherd-king, functions or missions echoed in the life of the Church as a whole and in the life of each and all of the baptised in particular. The value of this translation of *'munus'* in the encyclical would be to underline especially the participation of married couples who are baptised in such a mission, as part of their specific Christian vocation. However, Paul VI addressed this encyclical also to all people of good will and expressly stated that its teaching was based in part on natural moral law; in other words it was directed also to those in non-sacramental marriages. With full respect for the concept of 'mission', I have chosen to render *'munus'* as 'responsibility' in most instances, since this is what the text certainly means and since it applies to spouses both of whom are baptised and yet retains this broader reference to other spouses, too.

It has to be recognised that the issues addressed by Paul VI in this encyclical are complicated and controversial. Some of the terminology and analysis in the encyclical

---

[1] Cf. J.E. Smith, *Humanae Vitae: A Generation Later* (The Catholic University of America Press, Washington, D.C., 1991), 136-140; idem, "The Importance of the Concept of *'Munus'* to Understanding *Humanae Vitae*", in J.E. Smith (ed.), *Why Humanae Vitae was Right: A Reader* (Ignatius, San Francisco, 1993), 305-24.

itself, therefore, is somewhat technical. It would have been untrue to the text and unfair to Pope Paul, as well as to the Church as a whole, to over-simplify and so to distort what was written. It is hoped that the commentary will help to shed some light upon the problems tackled and especially upon the teaching given.

I have taken the unusual step of introducing additional numbers (1) and (2) in a key section of n. 14 (§ 4). This is due to the line of argument being put forward there, which has distinct parts to it, but where the distinction and the inter-relationship between them could not easily be brought out in another way.

I am indebted to Sister Assumpta, F.M.D.M., for checking my translation and for the corrections and many helpful suggestions she made. Any errors which remain are my own responsibility.

Translation

The Acts of Pope Paul VI
The Encyclical Letter 'Humanae vitae'

Given to our Venerable Brother Patriarchs, Archbishops, Bishops and Ordinaries of other places, retaining peace and communion with the Apostolic See, to the Clergy and Christian Faithful of the whole Catholic world and also to all people of good will: On the right ordering of the propagation of human children.

Pope Paul VI:

Venerable Brothers and Beloved Children, Health and Apostolic Blessing.

1. § 1 The very serious responsibility of transmitting human life, on the basis of which spouses give their free and conscious cooperation to God the Creator, has always bestowed on them great joys. These joys, however, carry with them at times not a few difficulties and trials.

   § 2 If discharging this responsibility has presented pressing questions for the conscience of spouses in every age, still the recent development of human society has

COMMENTARY

1. The first sentence of the text of the encyclical states clearly what it is about: the transmission of human life. Until the late 1970s, with the exception of the miraculous conception of Jesus, human life could only be transmitted through an act of sexual intercourse. Paul VI, however, immediately situated its transmission within the context of marriage by speaking of 'spouses'. Across the centuries Church teaching and people generally had recognised that marriage was the only proper setting for the generation of children. The care, feeding, clothing and shelter needed by children, as well as their moral and religious upbringing, requires a long period of time and the collaboration of both parents.[1] This is so even if single parents, in situations of abandonment, or of the grave illness

---

[1] Cf. St Thomas Aquinas, *Summa theologiae*, Supplement, q. 41, a. 1; q. 65, aa. 1-2.

brought about changes of such an order that new questions have arisen. These questions are connected with matters of great relevance to human life and happiness and the Church cannot ignore them.

or death of a spouse, are to be admired for striving to fulfil this task of love on their own.

The transmission of human life is not spoken of reductively, as if it concerned mere 'reproduction'. God is the source of all life, including human life. In what is an act of 'procreation', spouses are not, on their own, the source of new human life; they collaborate with God to bring that life into the world. Of course, the transmission of all forms of life follows God's plan in creation, but even animals operating by instinct are not to be compared with spouses, human beings, who by their 'free and conscious' activity, by rational, deliberate decisions, cooperate with God in a uniquely privileged way in the transmission of human life. This 'free and conscious cooperation' does not imply that a married couple are necessarily thinking of this directly in an act of their love, but that they perceive their marriage and their conjugal acts as involving such a collaboration, that this is part of the 'very serious responsibility' they accept in marriage and in these acts.[2]

Children are not seen primarily as a burden or a problem; they bring 'great joys'. It is not pretended that there are no difficulties or questions associated with marital life. These there had always been, but 'new questions' had included the regulation of birth, focused by the discovery of the anovulant

---

[2] The word *'munus'* means 'task', 'responsibility' or 'mission'. J.E. Smith has chosen to translate it almost always as 'mission': J.E. Smith, *Humanae Vitae: A Generation Later* (Catholic University of America Press, Washington, D.C., 1991), 137-138. This would be in keeping with its use in the Second Vatican Council where the threefold mission of Christ as Priest, Prophet and King is signalled by this word and where that threefold mission is recognised as pertaining to the Church. It can also indicate the vocation of Christian spouses in marriage, as the Council also shows. However, Paul VI's encyclical is addressed to all people of good will and deliberately refers to natural moral law, by which it is recognised that anyone whose moral reason and conscience are correctly attuned can in principle perceive the truth of what is taught here. Thus, it seems to me that, while 'mission' evokes the Christian vocation to marriage, 'responsibility' captures better the broader scope of the encyclical and perhaps stands a better chance of being seen by people generally as directed also to them.

I

*(New Aspects of the Problem and the
Competence of the Magisterium)*

2. § 1 For in truth the changes which have
occurred are both of great moment and of
different kinds. It is a question in the first
place of the rapidly increased number of
births, on account of which many fear that
the population of human beings may grow
more quickly than the means of sustaining
life may allow. They fear, in addition, that so
many families and so many peoples, striving
for progress, may be troubled as a result
by even greater pressures. For this reason
public authorities can easily be driven to the

pill. Earlier in the century, the fact of cycles of fertility and infertility in the menstrual cycle had been discovered, which had raised the question of 'natural methods' of regulating birth. Use of these by married couples for serious reasons had already been recognised as morally legitimate by Pius XII.[3] Moreover, although Magisterial teaching (that of the Pope and of the Catholic Bishops) on marriage had been positively presented in many respects by Pius XI and Pius XII, there had been a growing recognition of the desirability of attending directly to the role of conjugal, or marital, love in that teaching. This had been done at the recent Second Vatican Council, where the importance of procreation had also been underlined.[4] Nevertheless, the Council had not settled the precise question which Pope Paul was tackling in this encyclical, since he had made it clear that it was to be reserved to him as Pope. These inter-related developments had led to many expectations, particularly as marriage and what was morally right within marriage affected the lives of vast numbers of people across the world. All of these new dimensions affected the question being addressed now by the Pope.

2. The concerns of many people that the world's population was increasing so rapidly that it would impose a severe strain on resources and might reach the point where it would become unsustainable were serious. Such a fear had been noted in a classic text by the Anglican minister, Thomas Malthus, in 1798, that population increase was likely to proceed not in arithmetic (1, 2, 3, 4 ...), but in geometric (1, 2, 4, 16 ...) progression, so that food supplies would not be able to keep pace with it.[5] Such conjectures have often been taken as if they were scientific fact, when actually scientific

---

[3] Cf. Pius XII, Allocution to Participants at the Conference of Italian Mid-wives, *A.A.S.*, XLIII, (1951), 838-852.

[4] Cf. Second Vatican Council, Pastoral Constitution on the Church in the Modern World, *Gaudium et spes*, nn. 48-50.

[5] Cf. Rev. Thomas Malthus, *An Essay on the Principle of Population and on its Effects on Human Happiness* (London, 1798).

point where they wish to remove this sort of danger by rather more drastic means. It reaches the point where not only working and housing conditions, but also expanding needs, whether in the economic sphere or in terms of the upbringing and education of the young, affect the very status of human life, in which it may be often difficult today properly to look after the interests of a larger number of children.

and technological progress made more resources available to larger populations, whether dispersed more broadly or concentrated more densely.[6] Here Paul VI correctly notes people's worries not only about the long-term survival of the human race on earth, but about the quality of life, the standard of living, which may be endangered by a very large growth in population. The mention that developing countries may suffer especially badly, their progress being jeopardised, is significant not least because Pope Paul had himself issued an encyclical on human development, or progress, only the year before.[7] There is no doubt that the pressure of population growth provokes major problems in large cities of Asia and Latin America and in other areas.[8] However, the key problem is the allocation of research and resources, in that vast sums of money spent on armaments and on wars could do much to relieve shortages, as the Church's Magisterium recognised before and since 1968.[9] The United Nations, also, lamented the waste of resources on armaments.[10] On the other hand, the intervening decades since 1968 have seen a drastic implosion of birth rates in many Western countries to the point where the indigenous population will not be able to assure its survival and where a much reduced working population will find it increasingly difficult to support larger and longer-surviving, ageing communities.[11] Population pressure is one

[6] Cf. H.F. Smith, "The Proliferation of Population Problems" in J.E. Smith (ed.), *Why Humanae Vitae was Right: A Reader* (Ignatius, San Francisco, 1993), 385-403, esp. 385-390; hereafter *Why Humanae Vitae was Right.*

[7] Paul VI, Encyclical letter, *Populorum progressio*, 26 March, 1967, n. 37.

[8] Cf. John Paul II, Encyclical letter, *Sollicitudo rei socialis*, 30 December, 1987, n. 25.

[9] Cf. *Gaudium et spes*, n. 81; Paul VI, *Populorum progressio*, n. 53; John Paul II, *Sollicitudo rei socialis*, nn. 20, 24; idem, Encyclical letter, *Centesimus annus*, 1 May, 1991, n. 18.

[10] Cf. Report of the United Nations Commission on Research on Independent International Development, chaired by West German Chancellor, W. Brandt, *North-South: A Programme for Survival (1980) – The Brandt Report* (United Nations, New York, 1980), nn. 117-123.

[11] Cf. John Paul II, *Sollicitudo rei socialis*, n. 25; idem, Encyclical letter, *Evangelium vitae*, 25 March, 1995, nn. 16-17; H.F. Smith, "The Proliferation of Population Problems", in J.E. Smith, *Why Humanae Vitae was Right*, 389-392.

§ 2 It is also to be pointed out how our understanding has changed of the person of woman and of her role in human society and also, over and above this, of the value of conjugal love in marriage and of how conjugal acts are to be judged, if we look at them on the basis of that love.

§ 3 Then, it is especially to be noted that human beings have made such marvellous progress in regard to the forces of nature, both in subduing them and in arranging them skilfully according to their reason, that they attempt to extend this domination to the whole of their life, that is to their body, to the powers of their mind, to social life, to the very laws which govern the propagation of life.

factor in development, but it is ambivalent; it should not be used to foster practices which violate the dignity of the human person.[12]

The changed situation of women in society, in marriage and in regard to the implications of conjugal love is noted, but not elaborated. It can be inferred that the less docile place of women generally is in mind, the fact that already many wives were pursuing careers or having to work outside the home, that they had begun to hold important positions in politics, and such like. The call for women to be treated socially and politically as full equals of men was recognised and in some areas already advanced. Within marriage, such developments would imply changes as to who earned more or did the housework and cooking, cared for the children more directly, etc. The traditional framework could not be taken for granted any more. What impact all of this might have on the question of conjugal morality, including whether and how couples might judge in conscience to gauge whether or not they should seek more children, was highly relevant to the issue Pope Paul was addressing in this encyclical.

The further dimension noted that progress in dominating the forces of nature by virtue of human reason was leading some to want to extend that control to every area of life, including that of the human body and of procreation. The Second Vatican Council had spoken about progress or development in very positive terms. It had articulated a critically important principle, taken up by Paul VI in *Populorum progressio* in 1967 and in all the major social encyclicals of Popes since, namely that progress or development could not be measured simply on the basis of producing and of having more resources, although this was an important factor, especially in under-developed countries where life was in danger. The scandal of the rich growing richer and of the poor growing poorer discloses the truth that true or 'authentic human development' occurs when people become more fully human in all the

---

[12] Cf. Pontifical Council for Justice and Peace, *Compendium of the Social Doctrine of the Church* (Libreria editrice Vaticana, 2004), n. 483.

3. § 1 From this state of affairs new questions emerge. (It is asked) whether by reason either of the conditions of life as they now are or of the meaning which acts of conjugal intercourse have in safeguarding harmony and mutual fidelity between the spouses, it may not be appropriate to reconsider the moral norms which obtain at present. This is especially so if it is held that they can be observed only in the face of grave difficulties, at times with heroic sacrifice.

§ 2 Besides, (it is asked) whether the so-called principle of totality, addressed to this issue, may not allow it to be judged that a plan for a fecundity which is less fruitful, but more consonant with reason,

aspects of their being, 'being more' and not just 'having more' (the principle of the 'hierarchy of values').[13] We may say: 'who a person is' is more important than 'what a person has' or 'persons' are more important than 'things'.

As regards birth regulation, there was perhaps an assumption that scientific and technical discoveries which might facilitate a greater degree of control over the human body ought simply to be employed to curtail the population or to facilitate some other objective judged as valuable. Authentic human development does not mean rejecting scientific or technological progress, but demands that research be conducted in a morally upright way, for morally good purposes and be put only to morally good use. We should not simply assume that what becomes possible is to be used to achieve what we want to achieve ('I want, I can, I do'); we need to ask the properly moral question ('ought I to do that?').[14]

3. In this key section some new forms of moral argumentation, proposed by some Catholic moralists and advanced also at meetings of the Papal Commission on population and on the regulation of birth are examined.

The new arguments mentioned were the following:

    a. The pressing circumstances under which many married couples had to live were such that moral norms taught by the Magisterium, "the moral norms which obtain at present", could be observed only at "great inconvenience" or required "heroic sacrifice" and so it was asked whether it "may not be appropriate to reconsider" them (n. 3 § 1).

    b. Instead of looking at each and every individual conjugal act of the married life, if the marriage had been or were to be fruitful as a whole or 'in its totality', individual

---

[13] Cf. *Gaudium et spes*, n. 35.
[14] Cf. D. Tettamanzi, *Bioetica: nuove sfide per l'uomo* (Piemme, Casale, 1987), 31-33.

may be able to turn an act physically inducing sterility into a licit and prudent limitation of the generation of children. That is to say that (it is asked) whether it may not be right to consider that the end of procreating children belongs rather to the life of the spouses as a whole than to each of the individual (conjugal) acts which are part of it. Furthermore, they ask whether it is not the case, by reason of the awareness in conscience of their duties which people of today enjoy in greater measure, that the time has already come for the responsibility of handing on human life to be attributed rather to their reason and will than to certain (biological) changes of their bodies.

acts which were rendered sterile at other times might be morally licit, allowable (n. 3 § 2). The text refers to the "so-called principle of totality"; the principle of totality as such was a long-standing principle of moral theology, going back to St Thomas Aquinas, according to which a part might be sacrificed for the good of the whole, as when a gangrenous limb is amputated to save a person's life. It had been taught also by Pius XI and Pius XII. The latter had restricted its operation to organisms where the parts were physically united to the whole in a person's body, excluding its application to moral entities where the parts were connected to the whole only by a common intention or purpose. Thus, it was not to be applied to a society or to a country, with an individual person or citizen suffering bodily mutilation for the 'good' of the State, of some group or of some other person. This restriction Pius XII had introduced after the abuses of Nazi doctors using human beings as expendable objects of medical experiments for the 'good' of the purity of the Aryan race.[15] Paul VI's encyclical here uses the expression "so-called principle of totality" because what was being proposed was an entirely new and radically different version of the principle of totality. Some theologians suggested that individual conjugal acts which were contracepted might not be immoral, if the couple had been or would be open to new life in other conjugal acts during their marriage in its totality.[16]

---

[15] The Nazis had not invoked St Thomas. Pius XII wished to prevent abusive interpretations and applications of a legitimate and important principle; cf. Allocution to the Congress on Histopathology of the Nervous System, 13 September, 1952, *A.A.S.*, 44 (1952), 787-788.

[16] Cf. the so-called 'Majority Report' of the Papal Commission on Family, Population and Birth Regulation: "Documentum syntheticum de moralitate regulationis nativitatum" (Documentum A) in L. Rossi (ed.), *Controllo delle nascite e teologia: il dossier di Roma presentato e commentato da J-M. Paupert* (Queriniana, Brescia, 1967), part III ('principium generale' and 'nota explicativa'), 157; original French J-M. Paupert (ed.), *Contrôle des naissances et théologie: le dossier de Rome* (Seuil, Paris, 1967). Rossi correctly states

c. Part of the argument just outlined in b. makes a distinction between an act "physically" inducing sterility and the morality of the action of the couple more broadly. This would be to suggest that a contraceptive act might be physically contraceptive, but not morally so, on the basis of this new view of totality.[17] The idea was that this view of totality might "turn an act" of 'merely physical' contraception into a morally upright act, one which was "licit and prudent" (n. 3 § 2). This would not only be justified, according to this new opinion, on the basis of totality, but because the couple's decision might be "more consonant with reason", related to the "prudent limitation of the generation of children". What is involved here is a new approach to analysing the morality of human acts, not just in respect of the totality of the life of the couple, but because a good intention, in pressing circumstances, might seem to 'justify' means, here a contraceptive act, previously always judged immoral in Magisterial teaching and in Catholic moral theology.

d. A further element of importance is the inter-relationship between human "reason" and the merely "physical" act of contraception or between the "awareness of conscience" and "certain (biological) changes" in the body (n. 3 § 2), a distinction presented as a difference between physical and biological processes on the one hand and rational and deliberate judgments of conscience on the other.[18] There is no doubt that morality has to do with deliberate judgments and actions. A mere reflex action or something being done in complete ignorance of its true implications is not a

---

that Paupert's commentary is a polemical one, from one who supported the majority report. The references here are to the text of that majority group as reproduced by Paupert (document A).

[17] Cf. ibid., 157-158, IV ('Critica moralia spectantia ad interventum humanum in conceptione'), n. 2b.

[18] Cf. ibid., 155-156, II ('Argumenta ex lege naturae systematice exponuntur'), nn. 2-4.

4. § 1 Certainly, questions of this kind have always demanded new and deeper consideration from the Magisterium of the Church regarding the principles of moral doctrine relating to marriage, which is rooted in the natural law and illustrated and enriched in divine revelation.

§ 2 No member of the Christian faithful may legitimately go to the point of denying that the interpretation of the natural moral law belongs to the Magisterium of the Church. For there is no doubt at all – as

moral act or a human act as such; it cannot be qualified as good or bad, right or wrong, praiseworthy or blameworthy, precisely because it was not deliberately performed. What was being proposed here was that people, acting deliberately, might recognise biological changes in the woman's cycle and act to stop them from functioning through a hormonal contraceptive, and that this might be morally justified for reasons of limiting births.

These inter-connected proposals were radical (cf. n. 6 below). Tensions over moral teaching at the time and since were not essentially a matter of dispute between moral theologians and Church Magisterium; they divided moral theologians among themselves over the nature of moral truth, which the Catholic Church has always taught is an objective truth. The crisis in moral theology, unleashed in the decades after *Humanae vitae*, seems to have resulted from an explicit or implicit rejection of the encyclical's doctrine and from pursuing criteria we see here in germ (n. 3 § 2). John Paul II sought to specify and clarify the fundamental principles of moral theology to combat confusion and error over moral truth.[19]

4. The issues raised so far relate obviously to Church doctrine on marriage and on conjugal morality. That doctrine was said to be "rooted in the natural law and illustrated and confirmed in divine revelation" (n. 4 § 1). We need to consider these two realities and how one relates to the other.

Divine revelation, what God has revealed to us, was identified by classical Protestantism with the Bible, with 'sola Scriptura' ('Scripture alone'). The Catholic Church rejected that position at the Council of Trent, insisting on both Scripture and the Tradition of the Church as ways in which God revealed his will; so too did the Second Vatican Council. Here the mystery of the saving truth which God revealed for our salvation was said to be rooted in the sacred Scriptures

---

[19] Cf. John Paul II, Encyclical letter, *Veritatis splendor*, 6 August, 1993, nn. 4-5, 29, 110-112.

our Predecessors have proclaimed time and again[1] – that Christ Jesus, when he shared with Peter and the other Apostles his divine power, and sent them to instruct all nations in his precepts,[2] instituted these very Apostles as the sure guardians and interpreters of the whole law relating to morals; that is, not only of the law of the Gospel, but also of the natural law. For the natural law also (i.e., as well as the law of the Gospel) declares the will of God, whose faithful observance is surely necessary to people for their eternal salvation.[3]

§ 3 Moreover, the Church has followed this command in every age, but in more recent times it has given consistent teaching more abundantly relating to the nature of marriage or to the correct use of conjugal rights or to the duties of spouses.[4]

---

[1] Cf. Pius IX, Encyclical letter, *Qui pluribus: Pii IX Acta*, I, pp. 9-10; St Pius X, Encyclical letter, *Singulari quadam, A.A.S.*, IV (1912), p. 658; Pius XI, Encyclical letter, *Casti connubii, A.A.S.*, XXII (1930), pp. 579-581; Pius XII, Allocution, *Magnificate Dominum* ad episcopos totius catholici orbi, *A.A.S.*, XLVI (1954), pp. 671-672; John XXIII, Encyclical letter, *Mater et Magistra, A.A.S.*, LIII (1961), p. 457.

[2] Cf. Mt. 28: 18-19.

[3] Cf. Mt. 7: 21.

[4] Cf. *The Roman Catechism of the Council of Trent*, part II, chap. VIII; Leo XIII, Encyclical letter, *Arcanum, Acta Leonis XIII*, II (1880), pp. 26-29; Pius XI, Encyclical letter, *Divini illius Magistri, A.A.S.*, XXII (1930), pp. 58-61; Encyclical letter, *Casti connubii, A.A.S.*, XXII (1930), pp. 545-546; Pius XII, Allocution to the Italian Bio-Medical Association of St. Luke, *Discorsi e radiomessaggi di S.S. Pio XII*, VI, pp. 191-192; Allocution to Participants in the Conference of the Association of Italian Catholic Midwives, *A.A.S.*, XLIII (1951), pp. 835-854; Allocution to the Conference of the Association called 'Family Front' and to the Association of Large Families, *A.A.S.*, XLIII (1951),

or transmitted in the Church's Tradition, which are therefore normative for all Christians. Revelation is more than those words; it is everything God chose to make known to us for our salvation, completed in the very mystery of Jesus Christ, the fulness of revelation, in all he said and did. That revelation is transmitted or handed on in the Church's Tradition, in its teaching, liturgy and moral life.[20]

Thus, the moral teaching of the Scriptures includes marriage between one man and one woman as part of God's good creation and plan "from the beginning" and as a reality established by God: "what God has joined together ..." (Mt. 19: 6; Mk. 10: 9), a reality by which "each man has his own wife" and "each wife her own husband" (1 Cor. 7: 2-3). It reflects the radical and demanding teaching of Jesus, which rejected all adultery and divorce, in all true marriages, even between non-Christians. There are Scriptural indications for the sacramentality of marriage: Christians should "marry in the Lord" (1 Cor. 7: 40), while a man and a woman, "washed with a form of words", reflect in their marriage the "union between Christ and the Church" (Eph. 5: 26-27, 32).

If marriage, even between non-Christians, is found in revelation, to say it is "rooted in natural law" means that people who do not know or who do not accept revelation (i.e. God's will as revealed to Jews and to Christians), can nevertheless recognise the truth stated there 'naturally', through their own human reason, when it operates correctly ('right reason'). On that basis they can grasp the basic, intrinsic good of this life-long, faithful union of one man and one woman, open to life.

It might be thought that the encyclical approaches responsible parenthood mainly from a natural moral law perspective, referring to Scripture from time to time, to provide confirmation, greater clarity and depth, whereas the Council had urged that Scripture be the "very soul of all theology".[21] The encyclical was written in the light of the

---

[20] Cf. Second Vatican Council, Dogmatic Constitution on Divine Revelation, *Dei Verbum*, nn. 2, 4, 7.

[21] *Dei Verbum*, n. 24; cf. the Council's Decree on Priestly Training, *Optatam*

pp. 857-859; Allocution to the seventh International Conference of Haematologists, *A.A.S.*, L (1958), pp. 734-735; John XXIII, Encyclical letter, *Mater et Magistra, A.A.S.*, LIII (1961), pp. 446-447; Second Vatican Council, Pastoral Constitution, *Gaudium et spes*, nn. 47-52, *A.A.S.*, LVIII (1966), pp. 1067-1074; *Codex iuris canonici* (1917), cc. 1067, 1068 § 1, 1076, § 1-2.

Council's Scriptural, theological analysis (cf. n. 7 § 2) and did not need to repeat all it had said. The focus was on the core truths about marriage and about its moral requirements, truths central to the question of procreation and to the moral responsibilities entailed in it.

If it were argued that responsible parenthood was not directly treated in the Scriptures, although much directly relevant to it certainly is, the application of such teaching to responsible parenthood has to involve our moral reason; hence, some attention to natural moral law is needed. Previous Magisterium, in the texts listed in the footnotes to the encyclical, gives examples of this, teaching that marriage was divinely instituted, contraception was wrong, and natural rhythms could be used for serious reasons. The Second Vatican Council's pastoral, non-technical and theological teaching on marriage, marital love and responsible parenthood (not settling the matter of the pill) is part of that (n. 4 § 2).

There is a reassertion of the Magisterium's right to teach on these matters, whether known through revelation or through natural moral law. "No member ... of the faithful may ... deny" its right to interpret natural law, there being "no doubt at all" that Jesus intended the Apostles and their successors to be "guardians and interpreters" of the whole of divine law, including natural law, whose faithful observance "is surely necessary for ... eternal salvation" (n. 4 § 2). Simply expressed, doing what is right and good is necessary for salvation. Discerning right and wrong by our moral reason (natural law), even as to the application of what we may know from revelation, is important for believers. The Magisterium is to instruct and guide our consciences also here in the light of the Gospel.[22]

We need to say a little about what is meant by 'Magisterium' and about its role in moral teaching.

The Apostles, those who encountered the Risen Lord,

---

totius, n. 16.
[22] Cf. *Gaudium et spes*, n. 43.

HUMANAE VITAE: COMMENTARY

were appointed by Christ as his witnesses to proclaim and to hand on the saving truth of revelation (whose fulness is Christ and the whole of his saving mystery). Their successors, the bishops, also appointed by Christ, are to preserve and hand on this saving truth faithfully until the end of time. Thus, the bishops of the Catholic Church, united together and with the successor of Peter, the Pope, are charged by Christ with this Apostolic responsibility. Paul VI says that Christ Jesus shared with them "his divine power". Most translate this as 'authority' and it certainly includes the authority to preserve and transmit faithfully in teaching, moral life and liturgy, the whole, integral reality of revelation. Yet, 'power', here means more than 'authority'; it means 'sacred power' given to the Apostles when instituted by Jesus as such and given to their successors, the bishops, through their episcopal ordination or consecration directly by Christ to act in his name, through the sacraments. It includes authority, but that is tied to their being united also to one another in the 'communion' of the College of Bishops, with and never apart from the successor of Peter, the Pope. Only bishops of the Catholic Church form part of the College of Bishops.[23] Even a Catholic bishop not in full communion with the Pope is not part of the College of Bishops and so is not part of the Magisterium. This teaching authority of the College of Bishops is exercised ordinarily in their teaching around the world, but it can be exercised when they are together in a full Council (i.e. all Catholic bishops, with the Pope). It is reflected also in the Petrine ministry, where the Pope teaches as the successor of Peter, as the supreme pastor of the universal Church, the Church, throughout the world.

The authority bestowed by Jesus upon the Apostles and upon their successors to teach in his name or exercise teaching authority or 'Magisterium' (*'magister'*: 'master' or 'teacher')

---

[23] Cf. Second Vatican Council, Dogmatic Constitution on the Church, *Lumen gentium*, nn. 8, 15, 22; Congregation for the Doctrine of the Faith, Declaration on the Unicity and on the Salvific Universality of Jesus Christ and of the Church, *Dominus Iesus*, 6 August, 2000, nn. 16-17; idem, Responses to some Questions Regarding Certain Aspects of the Doctrine of the Church, 29 June, 2007, responses to questions 4 and 5.

5. § 1 In fact, led by an awareness of the same responsibility, we confirmed and expanded the Committee established by our venerable predecessor, John XXIII, in the month of March, 1963, which, besides many people who were experts in various disciplines relating to this matter, included also married couples. However, this committee was not looking at the matter only in order to examine advice and judgments concerning questions touching the conjugal life and particularly the correct norm for propagating children. Rather, over and above that, it was to refer its conclusions at the right time, so that the Magisterium of the Church might respond appropriately to the expectation by which both members of the Christian faithful and other people of the world were

remains at the service ('*ministerium*') of the Gospel or revelation. It is a necessary part of preserving and handing on what Christ intended for the salvation of all peoples. Although revelation concerns matters of faith, our response to God's call is not limited to truths of faith. As the Gospels show, the only response to Christ which is salvific is one which is not just a matter of words, but one which is lived out, one which concerns morals as well as faith. Not only religious moral duties (to pray, to receive the sacraments), but the pursuit of all moral duties rooted in basic human goods (not to kill, to be just, to be faithful in marriage, etc.) are requirements for believers, which apply to others too on the basis of what we call natural moral law. Paul VI recalled this task of teaching on morals, even of natural moral law, as part of the mission given to him by Christ (n. 4 § 2).

5. At this point the Pope speaks about advice and information provided to him by others, relevant to the serious question over "conjugal life and in the first place the norm for propagating children" (n. 5 § 1). Two particular sources of advice and information are mentioned, the Commission established by John XXIII and expanded by Paul VI, and also the bishops. Some bishops had been asked to provide advice and opinions on detailed aspects of the questions being examined and others had written with their views of their own volition (n. 5 § 2). This question had been under discussion at the time of the Second Vatican Council and it was easy for bishops then and later to express their thoughts. The Commission on Population, Family and Birth had consisted of "experts in various disciplines" relevant to marriage and procreation (doctors, psychologists, economists), including theologians, but there were also married couples there.

The role of this Commission was an advisory one, as Paul VI emphasises. Its members were "to examine advice and judgments" on marriage and on procreation, but the Commission was "to refer its conclusions" to the Magisterium, so that the Magisterium could give an authoritative response to those questions (n. 5 § 1). It had never been intended that

captivated about this matter.[5]

§ 2 Having received the conclusions of the investigations of the experts, and also opinions and advice from many of our brothers in the episcopate, sent to us in part of their own volition, in part as sought by us, this allowed us to evaluate more diligently all the parts of the argument in its details. For this reason we offer our most grateful thanks to all of them.

6. § 1 Nevertheless, the conclusions which the committee had reached could not be judged by us to bear the force of a certain and definitive judgment and to be such as to free us from our duty of clarifying a question of such great moment by a consideration of our own. Among the factors requiring

---

[5] Cf. Paul VI, Allocution to the Sacred College of Cardinals, *A.A.S.*, LVI (1964), p. 588, Allocution to the Commission on Population, Family and Birth, *A.A.S.*, LVII (1965), p. 388; Allocution to the Conference of the Association of Italian Obstetricians and Gynaecologists, *A.A.S.*, LVIII (1966), p. 1168.

the Commission would take a decision on the matter and it would be entirely wrong to imagine that Paul VI had a different approach here from that of John XXIII.

What is morally right and wrong cannot be settled by majority opinion; that would be to lapse into sheer relativism, implying that what was entirely right at one time was entirely wrong at another simply by reason of majority opinion. Nor was it pointless or misleading for the Popes to have called such a Commission together and then not to have followed its majority view. The Magisterium often seeks advice on technical aspects of moral questions from regular or occasional 'consultors' and 'experts', advising the Congregations and other offices of the Holy See on a range of doctrinal, ecclesial and moral issues with which they have to deal. In this case, the form of consultation was more publicly evident and relevant technical information would have included perhaps how the anovulant pill might function, the impact of pregnancy on underlying medical conditions, aspects of population pressures, etc. Experts and consultors are not as such members of the Magisterium. Thus, the Commission advised the Magisterium, but only the Magisterium has the competence and responsibility to teach authoritatively on the moral questions involved in the name of Christ, in the light of revelation and in the area of natural moral law.

6. The conclusions of the Papal Commission on Population, Birth and Family "could not be judged ... to bear the force of a certain and definitive judgment" (n. 6 § 1). This was partly because "full agreement about the moral norms to be proposed was lacking", but "especially because certain ways and reasons given of resolving the question emerged which departed from the doctrine on matrimony put forward with firm constancy by the Magisterium of the Church" (n. 6 § 1).

The Commission, in fact, had been so divided that it had issued two reports to the Pope. The majority report advocated a change in the moral doctrine, which would have allowed

such a consideration was also the fact that full agreement of opinions about the moral norms to be proposed was lacking in the committee and especially because certain ways and reasons given of resolving the question emerged which departed from the moral doctrine on matrimony put forward with firm constancy by the Magisterium of the Church.

§ 2 For this reason, having carefully examined the proposals put to us, having reflected on the matter diligently in mind and in soul, and having implored God with assiduous prayers, in virtue of the mandate entrusted to us by Christ, we now judge it right to give a response to the serious questions on this matter.

the use of contraceptives where there were grave reasons stemming from the woman's health or severe economic pressures or more generally from population pressures in a given area, making the raising of more children in the family very hard. This would not have been limited to the use of the anovulant pill and, for that reason alone, it would have entailed a real change, not just a development, in the moral teaching or doctrine given across the centuries and reaffirmed by recent Popes.[24] The other challenge to the Church's constant doctrine (cf. n. 3), concerned ways of discussing moral norms (expressing the good to be done and the wrong to be avoided) which would have implied a moral relativism, that what of its nature is morally wrong might be done legitimately, at least in some circumstances.

Pope Paul VI considered, then, that he had a duty to reflect on the matter himself (n. 6 § 1), "diligently" and in prayer. His duty stemmed from "the mandate entrusted to us by Christ", clearly referring to the mandate to Peter and to his successors and so to himself as Pope, as the supreme pastor of the universal Church. His "response to the serious questions on this matter" was given "in virtue of (that) ... mandate" (n. 6 § 2).

It should not be thought that this implies that the doctrine of the Church's Magisterium prior to this encyclical had been 'in doubt'. We might summarise the situation in this way. The centuries-old condemnation of contraception had been that of all Christian Churches and ecclesial communities until the Anglican Lambeth Conference of 1930 had claimed that it might be licit in some circumstances. The fact that this was constant doctrine was confirmed by the Greek Orthodox patriarch, Athenagoras, in 1968 after Paul VI issued this encyclical, saying: 'The Pope could not have expressed any

---

[24] Cf. "Documentum syntheticum de moralitate regulationis nativitatum" (Documentum A) in J-M. Paupert (ed.), *Il dossier di Roma*, 153-159, IV. "Criteria moralia circa spectantia ad interventum humanum in conceptione", nn. 3-4 at 158-159.

other doctrine'.[25] Pius XII had taught that using the newly discovered 'natural family planning' could be morally upright, if there were grave reasons justifying it, but he had reiterated the complete condemnation of all contraception. (It should be noted that the use of the natural cycle for grave reasons is in no way contraceptive.) In fact, Paul VI himself had expressly asserted that there was not a doubt of law about Church doctrine in this area only a few years before.[26] What was new was the anovulant pill and the question being addressed in these years could be put like this: did this fall under the moral norm articulating the condemnation of contraception or did it not? This was a new dimension of the moral life of spouses, which was specifically at stake in this encyclical. The opinion offered by the majority group of the Commission "did ... not bear the force of a certain and definitive judgment" (n. 6 § 1); in other words, this opinion itself was to be judged doubtful for the reasons outlined.

The Pope's duty as the successor of St Peter caused him to reflect on the matter diligently. To teach in the name of Christ and with the assistance of the Holy Spirit on moral matters does not mean that the Pope should await a blinding flash in the night or some other extraordinary phenomenon. Although there is not a canonical prerequisite such that subsequent teaching would not be valid without this, there is nonetheless a moral responsibility for the Pope to engage in such reflection, perhaps to seek advice, as he did in this case, and to attend to it once proffered (which does not mean to agree with it). This would be so also on the basis that the Magisterium has a moral responsibility to try to

---

[25] Cf. Statement of Athenagoras, Patriarch of the Greek Orthodox Church, after the encyclical, *Humanae vitae*, 1968. A. Günthör, "La dottrina della 'Humanae vitae' e il parere di rappresentanti di altre comunità cristiane" in AA.VV. (a cura di), *Humanae vitae: 20 anni dopo: Atti del II Congresso internazionale di teologia morale, Roma 9-12 novembre, 1988* (Ares, Milano, 1989), 515-527 at 517; my translation of Günthör's Italian version of the text.

[26] Paul VI, Allocution to Italian Obstetricians and Gynaecologists, 29 October, 1966, *A.A.S.*, 58 (1966), 1166-1170 at 1168-70.

II

(Doctrinal Principles)
(A Global Vision of the Person)

7. The question of propagating children, no differently from any question affecting human life, is to be examined beyond some particular points of view of the same kind as those which are called biological or psychological or demographical or sociological. It is to be examined in such a way that it embraces the whole person and the whole vocation to which he or she is called, which relates not only to natural and earthly matters, but also to supernatural and eternal aspects. Since there are many who undertake to defend artificial ways by which the number of children may be restricted and since these same people in this context put forward requirements of conjugal love or of the duty of responsible parenthood, so it is necessary to define and to explain carefully these two major elements of matrimonial life. This we shall

make its teaching understandable, to try to foster a response of acceptance.[27] However, the truth of a doctrine which is taught does not depend strictly on the reasons offered in support of it. The call to study the matter further, in its scientific and theological aspects (nn. 24, 28), was designed to help people to grasp and to follow the doctrine in their lives, in no way implying falsity or doubt as to the truth of the doctrine itself.

This first section concludes with the Pope stating unambiguously that he was now to give a response to the serious questions raised; in other words, he was to teach doctrine on this matter as Pope, as the supreme pastor of the universal Church.

7. In this first paragraph of what is often called the doctrinal section of the encyclical, the pressures on couples are recalled. It is noted correctly that those favouring contraception often base their arguments upon claims rooted in the concepts of conjugal love and of responsible parenthood, which, therefore, were to be analysed (cf. nn. 8-10 of the encyclical). This plan of what is to come is linked to a statement of intent, that this analysis will be conducted in the light of the doctrine of the Second Vatican Council on marriage and the family, which it had taught, says Paul VI, "with supreme authority" (n. 7). This it could do as a full (ecumenical) Council of the College of Bishops (not just a representation of them in a consultative gathering, as in the post-Conciliar Synods of Bishops). The Pope's express recognition of that doctrine and of its status and his express intention of evaluating conjugal love and responsible parenthood in the light of that doctrine should be noted. Far from there being any intention to retreat from the doctrine of the Council, the encyclical was to root its doctrine in that of the Council.

The opening sentence of this paragraph merits attention as

---

[27] Cf. J. Alfaro, "Theology and Magisterium" in R. Latourelle and G. O'Collins (eds), *Problems and Perspectives in Fundamental Theology* (New York, 1982), 340-356.

do in a sound manner, recalling those points particularly to mind which the Second Vatican Council recently expounded with supreme authority about this matter in its Pastoral Constitution issued under the words with which it begins, *Gaudium et spes* (Joy and Hope).

an expression of intent to assess the matters under discussion from the standpoint of the whole person and of the vocation, temporal and eternal, of the person. The Pope lists the dimensions of the serious questions being confronted as they were often put in discussion in the media, in terms of biology, sociology and psychology, without denying the importance of any of these. Yet, the insistence that the question of marriage and especially of responsible parenthood be considered, as with any other question concerning human life, "beyond (such) particular points of view ... in a way which embraces the whole person and the whole vocation" of the person (n. 7) is of fundamental significance.

This is itself an allusion to Conciliar doctrine, although no reference is given.[28] The Council taught that the human person is "one in body and spirit", sometimes loosely and inaccurately translated as 'made up of body and spirit'. It means that the human person, man in the generic sense, whether male or female, is inseparably one living reality here on earth until the time of death, inseparably a bodily and a spiritual being. This has major implications over the whole area of morality, since someone's body shares in the dignity of his or her person and is not a sub-personal reality or 'thing' at the disposal of the 'person', as if the 'person' were only identifiable with his or her spiritual or rational dimensions. Put more simply, the body is part of *who* the person is, <u>not</u> some-*thing which* the person has. This way of understanding the human person, which stems from the unique dignity of the person created in the image and likeness of God (Gen. 1: 26-27) and called to eternal redemption in Christ, is rooted in revelation, but it can be appreciated or grasped as true even by those who do not share our faith, on the basis of natural moral law. Morally, it implies that the human person ought never to be treated as an object, but only and always as an end, as intrinsically valuable. This key anthropological truth (Greek, *'anthropos'*: 'man' or 'human being', male or female), asserted by both the Council and by Paul VI, means that this and all moral issues

---

[28] Cf. *Gaudium et spes*, n. 14.

are not to be based on partial, limited perspectives, but on this total or integral anthropology.

Where the person is regarded as only 'spirit' or really spirit, the body, sexuality and sexual acts end up being seen as less than truly human, as in some way inferior, negative or even sinful – positions condemned by the Church in past centuries and reaffirmed by Pius XII when he called conjugal acts "noble and honourable", a teaching repeated by the Second Vatican Council.[29] However, an equally reductive, partial and misguided anthropology considers the spiritual as not really part of our humanity, so that the person is seen as being only matter, body, sensuality. Other perspectives which are reductive and so inadequate are those which see the person as only a function of society or which reduce the person to a collection of feelings and emotions to be analysed psychologically, as if that were all he or she were, as if that were all that counted. Some recent approaches in moral theology have risked falling into these reductive categories. John Paul II in his catecheses on human love, often called the 'theology of the body' in English, challenged such inadequate and misleading approaches. In his major encyclical on the principles of moral theology, he reiterated and elaborated upon the truth that the human person is "one in body and spirit" to insist that human nature involves the bodily, sexual, social, psychological, rational and spiritual dimensions of the person together.[30] Only such an integrated anthropology or understanding of the human person can serve as a proper basis for evaluating what is right and wrong in regard to the various human goods, which as a whole make up the good of the person as such (the integral human good), and for acting accordingly.

Paul VI taught that the human person in his or her totality as a person, and in their vocation as a whole, was the only proper basis for evaluating the moral demands of marital or

---

[29] Cf. Pius XII, Allocution to Italian Midwives, 29 October, 1951, *A.A.S.*, 43 (1951), 838-852; Second Vatican Council, *Gaudium et spes*, n. 49.
[30] John Paul II, *Veritatis splendor*, n. 50.

(*Conjugal Love*)

8. § 1 In fact, then, conjugal love will reveal to us its true nature and nobility above all, if we think of it as if emanating as from that highest source, from God, who 'is Love'[6] and who is the Father, 'from whom all parenthood in heaven and on earth is named'.[7]

§ 2 Therefore, so much is missing where marriage is thought to be born from mere chance or from the blind course of natural forces, as in reality God the Creator

---

[6] Cf. 1 Jn. 4: 8.
[7] Cf. Eph. 3: 15.

conjugal love, and the question of conscious or responsible parenthood (n. 7). This does not deny the importance of the biological, sociological and psychological, nor of the rational and spiritual, but they need to be integrated. Some theologians and others have taken what the Pope says elsewhere in the encyclical out of context. As it is important to understand the context of a Biblical passage to interpret it correctly, it is important also to interpret a Papal encyclical in its proper context. Since Paul VI explicitly insists on an integral anthropology, it is a distortion of his teaching to pretend that he operates only or primarily from the standpoint of biology.[31] The integrated anthropology he espouses here, in full conformity with the Council, must be seen as a key for interpreting what he says later.

We can now turn to the two concepts which the Pope indicated need to be examined as a prelude to discussing the moral norms as such on procreation, namely conjugal or marital love, which he examines first in nn. 8-9, and then responsible parenthood, which he examines in n. 10, with some key remarks following in nn. 11-12.

8. Paul VI begins this reflection on conjugal love from a specifically theological perspective: God is love and the source of all love, and from God the Father derives the concept of parent (n. 8 § 1). He contrasts this with a view of marriage as "mere chance", stemming from the "blind course" of the natural powers of the human person (n. 8 § 2). 'Mere chance' and the 'blind' functioning of 'natural powers' or urges are reductive ways at looking at marriage; they undervalue it and rob it of meaning, leaving no place for human judgment.

One way of considering life generally, common in those years and by no means absent since, was that of existentialism, taking things as they are found, even the person, and in some versions considering everything as literally 'absurd', sheer

---

[31] This matter is examined in the general reflection on the encyclical in the appendices.

instituted it wisely and providently with the intention that he might bring about his plan of love in us. On account of this, through the mutual gift of self which is proper and exclusive to them, spouses pursue that communion of persons by which they perfect one another mutually, in such a way that they associate their action with God for the procreation and for the education and upbringing of new living beings.

§ 3 However, for those washed by sacred baptism, marriage of this sort is established with such a dignity that it exists as a sacramental sign of grace, since it designates the union between Christ and the Church.

chance and meaningless. Proponents of such theories often urged people to make up or construct their own sets of values as they saw fit and judged this to be the only way to live 'authentically'. One of the influences which has undermined the stability of marriage in recent decades has been such an attitude, perhaps not expressed in those terms, but adopted from popular presentations and from the media. It is true that much in life seems to be the effect of chance, where someone is born, whether, how and when people meet one another, what a person finds attractive or not, and so on. Yet, that is only part of the truth. The fundamental attraction of a man for a woman, leaving aside for the present anomalous situations, is found in the overwhelming majority of people and lies at the heart of the difference between the sexes or genders. Related to the structure of the DNA in the chromosomes in every cell of our bodies, it is not mere chance. Also rooted in such structures are our height, skin colour, colour of our eyes and hair, perhaps to some extent even levels of intelligence and interests of one sort or another and many other features which make us more or less attractive to others. Yet, these variations are variations within what is fundamental and common to all (our basic, essential nature), despite anomalies, disabilities, in individual cases. Beyond variations which 'happen' to be there in us and which affect our relationships with others, the underlying bodily, sexual, rational and spiritual dimensions which are part of our being human persons and which are common to all involve so many invariable, regular, explicable features that sheer chance cannot properly account for them. Even many factors which are unique to a person or which are present in a unique way in a person form part of the pattern of being human and often exercise an influence in bringing two people attracted to one another to realise that they love one another.

Even at the human level or from a natural law stance, the reality of marriage is seriously misrepresented if it is thought of as a matter of mere chance. Among the features which form part of our sexuality are the sexual urges and passions

which we experience and which are triggered in part by other specific persons. These, along with features of personality and character, are part of what may attract or repel people in complex ways. It would not be true to say that such passions, urges or 'natural forces' explain marriage, since people are not necessarily, and ought not to allow themselves to be, slaves of such passions. In the worst cases, where people do allow themselves to be dominated by such urges in their sexual behaviour, we characterise them rightly as behaving like animals. Human beings know that initial attractions are not yet that love which is truly marital. Getting to know one another's personalities, interests, families, etc., and developing friendship with them is properly part of seeing how deep a relationship is or might become. Here human reason is at work, not in a cold or repressive way, but in a responsible manner. Marriage is the work neither of mere chance nor of the blind operation of natural passions, but is a special type of relationship into which sexuality, passion, personality, shared interests and plans and the spirituality of the two persons concerned can flow and in which they are to be lived in a fully integrated and thus fulfilling way.

What Paul VI underlines here is that marriage is a reality full of genuine meaning, not a senseless product of absurd forces. It was instituted by God in his providence for our good, a good designated here as love: "to bring about his plan of love in us" (n. 8 § 2). While not all marriages are happy, even those who do not know God can see marriage as an institution with the capacity to foster love between a man and a woman in a way that no other relationship between two human beings can manage.

Paul VI defends the intrinsic meaning and good of marriage. God's plan of love in us in marriage involves the spouses in "the mutual gift of self which is exclusive to them". This love is neither a vague 'feeling', nor mere erotic passion (although it will integrate such passion), nor selfish calculation, and it is much more than an ordinary friendship. The Council had distinguished marital love from inadequate

notions of 'love' often found in society and had taught that it was a "mutually self-giving love". Paul VI fully endorsed the Council's development of doctrine and its important clarification on this point.[32]

This mutually self-giving love of the couple is "proper and exclusive to them" as spouses. This long-standing doctrine, expressed in these very terms in the Council, reinforces the unique nature of marriage as between one particular man and one particular woman.[33] It alludes also to the conjugal act as the act in which only married couples may engage (it is 'exclusive' to them) and in which they have a right and duty to engage (it is 'proper' to them). This recalls the Biblical teaching that a man leave his mother and father, cleave to his wife, the two becoming 'one flesh' (Gen. 2: 23-24; Mt. 19: 5; Mk. 10: 7; 1 Cor. 6: 16) and, further, that each man have his own wife and each woman her own husband, the two fulfilling their duty to one another (in the conjugal act), abstaining only by common agreement, for a time and for prayer, to avoid the danger of being tempted to seek satisfaction through adultery (1 Cor. 7: 2-5).

In the light of this doctrine on conjugal love and on the conjugal act, Paul VI teaches that both have a two-fold dimension or meaning, expressed through those conjugal acts. The spouses "pursue that communion of persons by which they perfect one another mutually" and they "associate their action with God for the procreation and education of new human beings" (n. 8 § 2). The Council had portrayed marriage as an "intimate partnership (communion) of life and love", the "good of the spouses" themselves being part of what marriage is about, and the conjugal act as a truly inter-personal act fostering their mutual perfection.[34] Here the Pope takes this further in that marriage and the conjugal act are seen as having the intrinsic meaning of nurturing a 'communion of persons', something he calls later the 'unitive meaning' of such acts. The other meaning intrinsic to marriage and to the

---

[32] Cf. *Gaudium et spes*, n. 49.
[33] Ibid.
[34] *Gaudium et spes*, nn. 48-49.

(The Characteristics of Conjugal Love)

9. § 1 Having situated these points in their proper light, both the characteristics proper to conjugal love and its specific requirements emerge clearly. It is of supreme importance to evaluate these in a way which recognises the proper value of each of them.

§ 2 This love, first of all, is clearly *human*; it is both perceptible to the senses and spiritual. For this reason, it does not involve only the urge of nature or of the passions, but also and especially it is operative in the act of free will, obviously with the orientation that, through the joys and sorrows of daily life, it not only may persevere, but besides that also increase. This it does in such a way that the spouses may truly become as

conjugal act is the 'procreative meaning' by which the couple cooperate with God in the bringing about of new life. The close connection between these two meanings is to be noted, since the conjugal act fosters the communion of persons "in such a way that" the couple's action is open to cooperation with God in procreation.

Where two baptised persons marry one another, the marriage is a sacrament and as such reflects the relationship between Christ and the Church (cf. Eph. 5: 21-33). Their marriage is not just called to be a sign of this relationship, but of its nature it is such, "a sacramental sign of grace" (n. 8 § 3). Clearly, the vocation of such a couple is to live their marriage in such a way that they do not contradict that sign by the way they live or behave, but rather in a way which is consonant with it.

9. The Pope had sought to evaluate the key characteristics of conjugal love and of responsible parenthood as a necessary step towards addressing the main question of the encyclical, the morality of the means of regulating births (n. 7). After insisting that marriage is not a matter of mere chance or passion, that it has true human meaning as both unitive and procreative, expressed through the conjugal act, he now summarises some of the key features of conjugal love, in line with Conciliar teaching.

Conjugal love is:

a. *human*: It is not just a question of impulses, urges of nature and of passions (cf. n. 8), but of acts of free will, directed to persevering through the joys and sorrows of every day life, directed to its own growth. It is not to be considered just from one perspective (biological, sociological, psychological, rational or spiritual), but as an integrated whole (n. 7). Erotic attraction, sexual impulses and passions alone or in isolation are not enough to constitute 'love', especially 'conjugal love', a truth believing Christians and all can see to be true, especially given the abuse, neglect, disregard and selfish manipulation of others which often occur in human sexual encounters.

one heart and one mind and at the same
time may obtain together (as one) their
perfection as human beings.

Although such acts would be human acts in the sense that they are deliberately undertaken and so can be evaluated morally (as morally wrong), they are not acts of properly human love, but quite the opposite. Marriage and the conjugal act imply mutual self-giving love, with full respect for the spouses involved as persons. As the Council had remarked:

> "... this eminently human (love) ... is directed by the affection arising from the will from person to person, ... embraces the good of the whole person, ... enriches the expressions of the body and of the mind with a special dignity and allows them to be ennobled as elements and signs of a special conjugal friendship."[35]

Paul VI's summary of this clearly human love causes him to add, in full conformity with the Council and with the Church's centuries-old doctrine, that it is to persevere and to grow. In other words, human beings are not properly treated as human beings when they use one another sexually in casual encounters. Perseverance means that the love of marriage is one which seeks to endure. As a love designed to grow, to be concerned with the good of each of the partners as such and with their mutual perfection, it implies husband and wife taking a mutual and genuine interest in one another's health, happiness, wishes and worries. That they should grow together in one heart and mind is not mere idealism; it is to be lived in the difficulties or sorrows of life, as well as in times of joy. Rather, it indicates that love, here marital love, of its nature tends to grow and blossom; since this does not occur automatically and much less where resisted, it implies a moral responsibility to commit themselves to one another in nurturing this love in what Paul VI would call its 'unitive' meaning, the meaning it has of its nature of uniting the couple more deeply to one another.

---

[35] *Gaudium et spes*, n. 49.

§ 3 Then it involves a love which is *full*, that is that it is a question of that peculiar form of personal friendship, in which the spouses share everything between themselves with a great generosity, in which they neither allow there to be unjust exceptions to this nor seek unduly their own convenience. Whoever loves their spouse truly, loves them in fact not so much for that which they receive from them, but loves them for themselves, and they do this willingly, so that they may enrich one another with the gift of themselves.

b. *full*: Marital or conjugal love involves friendship, which all of us need in life and which sustains us in many ways, but it is a special or peculiar form of friendship in that everything is to be shared whole-heartedly. This feature of the husband-wife relationship is what distinguishes marriage from other forms of friendship and from other forms of relationship. Obviously, some things one of the spouses is able to do and another not, given that as individuals they have different abilities and weaknesses, but conjugal love certainly implies that, in principle and as far as possible in reality, they cease to live two separate lives and live a 'common life' (what the Council called "an intimate community of life and love"[36]), sharing everything with one another. The addition that spouses should make "no unjust exceptions" to this "nor seek unduly their own convenience" takes account of what has just been said about personal capacities. Yet, it would mean that they should share their finances and resources, that one should not normally have separate bank accounts or keep a significant part of their life or their decisions secret from the other (saving exceptional circumstances where one of the spouses had a chronic problem of financial irresponsibility and the other sought to ensure payments of bills, etc., in a way which would be for the good of the couple as a couple, the family as a family, and not for private or selfish purposes). Decisions should be joint and should result from honest discussion. Seeking our own convenience is not necessarily wrong, but a married person doing this 'unduly' would be selfish and would neglect or harm their spouse and their marriage.

Love as 'full' entails loving the other spouse not for what can be received, but for their own sake (n. 8 § 3). The person of the spouse is intrinsically valuable, a good as such, is not to be reduced to a mere means of obtaining some other good.[37] Certainly, someone marrying wishes

---

[36] Ibid., n. 48.
[37] Cf. G. Grisez, *The Way of the Lord Jesus*, II, *Living a Christian Life* (Francis-

§4 In addition to this, conjugal love is *faithful* and *exclusive*, till the end of life, something clearly which the bridegroom and bride understood in their minds on that day on which freely and in clear awareness they gave themselves to one another in the bond of marriage. No-one, however, may claim to receive many benefits, wishes to become happy in marriage, and judges precisely that only in marrying this specific person of the opposite sex can they attain that happiness which they seek. Love in this sense is not just other-centred or altruistic (*'amor benevolentiae'* or *'agape'*), but each of the spouses rightly also wishes to share in the benefits or goods of that love (*'amor concupiscentiae'* or *'eros'*).[38] Yet, marital love is precisely and necessarily altruistic, in that it must seek the true good of the other spouse, as well as that of any children, willing to make great sacrifices, and across the years, for the person they love. This is why it is always important to be realistic, as well as idealistic, in preparing for marriage and in deciding to marry. Not just the obviously attractive elements, but the irritating features of the other person need to be recognised and evaluated. Where a couple love one another truly, their love is not based on illusion or self-deception, but they truly love the person as such, despite difficulties or flaws which all human beings possess; these are neither ignored nor minimised. Where a person in courtship is seriously irresponsible (financially, sexually, by violent behaviour, etc.) and cannot or will not change, it is very wrong to marry them, since on the part of the other there is not the reciprocity needed for marriage (the love is one-sided) and/or the one who 'loves' them can only love a part of them or loves an idealised version of this other. Flaws, differences and irritations which are not grave, but which are accepted as part of the other, can be accepted in genuine, married love.

c. *faithful and exclusive* until the end of life: The Latin text does not italicise 'until the end of life', but it might well have done so. Exclusivity means that one particular man has this unique relationship with one particular woman

---

can Press, Quincy, Illin., 1993), 557-569 on marriage as more than an instrumental good, but as an intrinsic and basic human good.

[38] Cf. Benedict XVI, Encyclical letter, *Deus caritas est*, 25 December, 2005, n. 7.

that this fidelity between spouses, even if at times it may have its difficulties, is not possible, since, on the contrary, in every age it is noble and full of benefits. For, as the centuries have gone by, the examples given by so many spouses not only prove this to be appropriate to the nature of marriage, but, furthermore, (show also) that their intimate and enduring happiness flows from this, as from its source.

and she with him; they are "non-substitutable persons" or are irreplaceable in marriage.[39] In other words polygamy (one husband with several wives) and polyandry (one woman with several husbands) are excluded of their nature by marriage, which is monogamic.[40] This element of marriage is that of 'unity'; it implies exclusiveness, such that no-one else can be admitted to the man-wife relationship as such, and it implies fidelity to one another, excluding adultery. This in no sense means that the couple or either one of them cannot love anyone else, nor that their marital love ought not to expand to embrace other people (conjugal love is not a form of joint selfishness or 'égoïsme-à-deux'), but it does exclude everyone else from the couple's relationship precisely as marital.

Paul VI focuses attention on the consent which brings marriage into being, since fidelity, exclusivity and indissolubility are part of what is understood by the spouses on their wedding day when they consent to marry one another "freely and in clear awareness" (n. 9 § 4). This does not mean that they have to have a technical knowledge of theology, but it does require that they have a basic grasp of these key features of marital love summarised here. Marriage preparation ought to help those courting one another or engaged to one another to appreciate what it is they are taking on in marrying one another, to ensure that they make their commitment of consent knowingly and freely.

The pressures of modern society and of the media suggest at times that fidelity, exclusivity and indissolubility might be nice ideals, but are actually impossible to realise or live out in practice. The difficulties can be very real and need not be rehearsed here, but the Pope simply states a truth, namely that very many couples across the

---

[39] Cf. W.E. May, *Sex, Chastity and Marriage: Reflections of a Catholic Layman, Spouse and Parent* (Franciscan Herald Press, Chicago, 1981), 86; idem, *Sex and the Sanctity of Human Life* (Christendom College Press, Fort Royal, Vir., 1984), 17-18, 44.

[40] Cf. Benedict XVI, *Deus caritas est*, n. 12.

§ 5 Lastly, this love is *fruitful*; the whole of this love is certainly not contained within the communion of the spouses alone, but it tends also to extend itself and to give rise to new lives. 'Marriage and conjugal love are ordered by their very nature to the procreation and education and upbringing of children. Children are surely the supreme gift of marriage and they contribute very greatly to the good of the parents themselves.'[8]

---

[8] Cf. Second Vatican Council, Pastoral Constitution, *Gaudium et spes*, n. 50, *A.A.S.*, LVIII (1966), pp. 1070-1072.

centuries have not only demonstrated that living out such commitments of conjugal love is possible, but have found happiness in doing so; indeed, their happiness, he claims, has flowed from the nature of marriage thus outlined and from the commitments they have made in these respects. This is not an idle claim; it is simply true that couples have enjoyed good and happy marriages, knowing they are mutually faithful in a unique relationship which is also an enduring one until death. The presuppositions of infidelity, of betrayal, of divorce if things do not work out, of 'contracts' as to what will happen when they do not succeed, are the very factors which undermine marriage, where suspicion and calculation replace trust and unconditional commitment.

d. *fruitful*: This dimension of conjugal love touches more directly upon the question of the encyclical on births and their regulation. It is not inserted here polemically, but to stress that conjugal love, like every other form of love whatever, is of its nature inherently fruitful. Love is not a static reality and it cannot be taken for granted. Either it is growing or it is weakening. The sadness of many married couples stems from their having neglected to nurture their love for one another and for their family, from having paid more heed to work and career to finance their lives and to furnishings in the house than to the person(s) for whom they have been working or for whom the house exists. Any love which is real tends of its nature to grow and to expand, even though it does not do so automatically. The couple have a moral responsibility to nurture their love for one another and its growth, including that of being open to the possibility of children.[41]

With marital love the particular dimension of fruitfulness which is the procreation of children is an inherent part of that love. Paul VI quotes the Second Vatican

---

[41] Cf. K. Wojtyla, *Fruitful and Responsible Love* (St Paul's, Slough, 1978), 18-22; I. Fuček, *La sessualità al servizio dell'amore: Antropologia e criteri teologici* (Dehoniane, Roma, 1993), 133-135.

(Responsible Parenthood)

10. § 1 For these reasons conjugal love demands from the spouses that they attend carefully to their responsibility regarding responsible parenthood which, since it is so strongly advocated today and with very good reason, is to be rightly understood. Hence, it is necessary that this be considered on the basis of various and legitimate factors, which are inter-connected with one another.

Council here, which recognised marriage and conjugal love as of their nature ordered to children and children as the supreme gift of marriage (n. 9 § 5). The yearnings of married couples to have children are entirely natural and good. The possibility afforded by our human nature for a man and a woman to have children together is a further indication not just of a biological possibility, but of this basic human good intrinsic to marriage and of God's providential plan not just for the survival of the human species in the abstract, but for the good or blessing of children (Gen. 1: 28).[42] The conjugal act itself is directed also to the procreation of children, a fact confirmed by those seeking to contracept, since they must recognise this inherent possibility in this unique act of making love (unique too since it is the only act by which they can express their love together which could have that possibility) or they would not seek to render it fruitless. Children are not a nuisance, an obstacle, a disease or a burden, but an inherent or intrinsic good of marriage; as the Council had taught, they are the supreme gift of marriage.[43]

10. Responsible parenthood is examined in this encyclical on the basis of a view of the human person considering all their essential dimensions (n. 7), and of the essential characteristics of conjugal love (n. 9). Many people asking the Church to reconsider its doctrine had genuine worries and anxieties (nn. 1-3). Entering the precise area the encyclical intended to treat, it is all the more important not to mis-read what is said.

Many people have thought that the Pope did not really appreciate the pressures on a woman from her health or the economic difficulties under which many families laboured or the population pressures. Many non-Catholics and quite a few Catholics think that he rejected the whole idea of

---

[42] Cf. Grisez, loc. cit., 569-571.
[43] Cf. *Gaudium et spes*, n. 50.

§ 2 If we think first of the biological processes, responsible parenthood means the knowledge and observance of the responsibilities relating to those processes, since, in the capacity for procreating life, human reason has detected biological laws which belong to the human person.[9]

---

[9] Cf. St Thomas, *Summa theologiae*, I-II, q. 94, a. 2.

'responsible parenthood' or, worse, that Catholics especially, but others too, were being asked to react to the question of the regulation of new births in a truly irresponsible way. It is particularly necessary to read what Paul VI said and not to rely upon popular presentations of his doctrine. Not only did he not reject responsible parenthood, he insisted on it, specifying the criteria to be adopted in its regard. We should note that he is not addressing the means which ought to be used in any depth, but is concerned above all with the couple's *intentions*. In later paragraphs (nn. 14-16) he turns to the means more directly.

The criteria for responsible parenthood, at the level of the couple's *intentions*, are not to be seen in isolation or the doctrine risks mis-interpretation; they "are inter-connected with one another" (n. 10 § 1).

a. *biological processes*: In relation to procreating human life, human reason grasps biological laws which belong to the person. These references to 'biological processes' and to 'biological laws' in the human person have been interpreted by some, including Catholic moral theologians, as suggesting that the Magisterium was saying that natural moral law means slavishly following biological laws involved in procreation just because they exist and work in a given way. The suggestion is that Paul VI took mere biology and made it a moral law.

If these interpretations were correct, they would not fit in with long-standing Catholic moral doctrine that we may use medicines to cure illnesses, that limbs may be amputated under the principle of totality, if they are so diseased as to threaten a person's life. We do not abandon ourselves to mere biological functioning, when life or health is in danger. That is not what Paul VI was saying. He had stated categorically, the question of responsible parenthood was not to be approached from a partial (biological) perspective, but from an integral perspective, that of the whole person (n. 7). Here he meant quite simply that couples should give due consideration to biological

§ 3 If, then, we look at impulses which are inborn and at passions of the soul, responsible parenthood makes clear the necessary control which reason and will ought to exercise over them.

processes or laws when forming their intention in regard to the procreation of children. This does not mean that they need a degree in biology before they can marry or before a married couple engage in the conjugal act. First of all, they need to know that marriage involves acts between them of an intimate sexual nature, that marriage is not a disembodied or merely Platonic relationship.[44] Secondly, they need to have a basic awareness of the fact that their acts can give rise to procreation at some times in the woman's cycle, but not at others. These factors are morally significant; the first concerns a dimension of how they ought to relate to one another as a married couple in general and the second ought to affect the decisions they make about when to engage in those intimate acts, partly also in terms of how the wife is feeling, but specifically as to whether these particular ways of expressing their love should be used at a given time or not.

b. *in-born passions*: As we have already seen, it is not a truly human way of behaving to allow ourselves to be carried along by our passions and urges, whether of a sexual nature or otherwise. Someone who is bad-tempered ought not to let himself or herself be carried away and give vent to their feelings in outbursts which are offensive or unjust. Animals are indeed beings which operate by mere instinct, but human beings ought to integrate their passions, good and bad, into a proper way of living orientated to the attainment of our full good, the enjoyment of God's beatitude or blessed joy for the whole of eternity. The sexual passion in itself is good, a natural inclination orientated to the procreation of children and also to the expression and deepening of a married couple's love for one another. The "necessary control which reason and will ought to exercise" (n. 10 § 3) over the sexual passions does not mean denying them

---

[44] Ignorance of this truth can occur, e.g., where someone has a seriously limited upbringing, but it is not to be presumed after puberty: *The Code of Canon Law* (1983), c. 1096 § 2.

§4 If after this we turn to physical, economic, psychological and social conditions, those are said to act with responsible parenthood who either, led by prudent consideration and generosity of spirit, decide to accept a greater number of children or who, for causes of a serious nature and observing the norms of morality, judge that they should not have another child either for a specific or for an indefinite period of time.

or repressing them, but channelling them into acts which are right and good and into a way of life which is morally responsible. The virtue of marital chastity involves the deliberate, constant pursuit of the true goods of marriage in this way.[45]

c. *physical, economic psychological and social conditions*: We can take the term 'physical' to refer in many instances to the health of the couple, perhaps especially of the wife who may have had difficult pregnancies before or who may have an illness which might make pregnancy dangerous to her health or even to her life. Economic conditions would certainly include the situation of the family, whether the couple judged that they could afford to have another child at present, but could refer to the conditions in the country where they lived, insofar as they might impinge upon their family. Psychologically, there is again a question of health, that of the couple's ability to embrace and rear another child. Social conditions might have to do with housing, availability of food, medical and perhaps social services.

Not only does Paul VI not ignore these factors, but he insists that they be examined by the couple in coming to a decision at the level of their intention as to whether or not they ought to seek another child at present. This does not mean that they have to examine all such factors every time that they might think of or wish to express their love for one another through the conjugal act. Not only would that deprive them of the spontaneity which is properly part of their lives, but it would not be practicable. They need to discuss these factors from time to time, to form a virtual, habitual intention about responsible parenthood, on the basis of which they are then able to act.[46]

---

[45] Cf. Pontifical Council for the Family, *The Truth and Meaning of Human Sexuality: Educational Guidelines for the Family* 8 December, 1995, nn. 16-18, 20; J. Grabowski, *Sex and Virtue: An Introduction to Sexual Ethics* (Catholic University of America Press, Washington, D.C., 2003), 85-89.

[46] Cf. G.E.M. Anscombe, *Contraception and Chastity* (C.T.S., London, undated), 25.

§ 5 Furthermore, that responsible parenthood of which we are speaking especially brings with it that other and intrinsic foundation, which pertains to the moral order which they call objective and which is established by God, of which the true interpreter is a correct conscience. For this reason the task of responsible parenthood demands that the spouses recognise their duties towards God, towards themselves, towards their family and towards human society, while observing the proper order of things and of goods.

§ 6 From this it emerges that in the responsibility of transmitting life it is not open to them (the spouses) to act on the basis of their own will, as if they were allowed to define the morally upright ways which they should follow in a completely free and autonomous fashion. Rather, they are obliged to adjust their behaviour to the

However, the answers are not to be presumed to point in one direction. The judgment formed in conscience at the level of intention is not automatically to be thought of as implying a restriction of the number of children. It may be that they should seek "a greater number of children", as in areas where now the indigenous population has decreased alarmingly or where economic factors are more positive. It may be that an honest and prudent judgment is that they should not seek another child for the time being or indefinitely (n. 10 § 4).

d. *recognition of their responsibilities and of the goods involved*: This evaluation in conscience has to consider:

– their duties towards God, themselves, their family, society, in light of the factors just noted (n. 10 § 5)

– the plan of God in marriage and in the conjugal act (n. 10 § 6); some key norms relating to this we have elaborated above (n. 9).

This judgment at the level of the intention should recall that children as such are good, that marriage is orientated to the procreation of children, as well as to deepening the union of the couple, both aspects of the vocation of Christian spouses and of any married couple's life.

e. *respect for the relevant objective moral norms*: Here we touch the question of means, but in very general terms. The role of conscience in regard to Magisterial teaching, specifically on the matter of marriage and responsible parenthood, will be examined in its own right.[47] Yet, it is the consciences of the spouses which have to examine these matters, to evaluate responsibilities. This the Second Vatican Council and also Paul VI had already

---

[47] See the general reflection on the encyclical in the Appendix.

plan of God the Creator, which, on the one hand, the very nature of marriage and of its acts expresses and which, on the other hand, the constant doctrine of the Church declares.[10]

---

[10] Cf. Second Vatican Council, Pastoral Constitution, *Gaudium et spes*, nn. 50-51, *A.A.S.*, LVIII (1966), pp. 1070-1073.

emphasised, when opposing governmental programmes of abortion and contraception.[48] Yet, it is not for the couple to make up the moral norms which they wish to follow; they are "not ... to act on the basis of their own will ... to define ... morally upright ways in a completely ... autonomous fashion" (n. 10 § 6). Here, as in all areas of life, objective moral norms express the truth of who we are and of what we are called to do. The Council's text had specifically insisted that this pertained to the properly formed consciences of the spouses respecting the demands of the moral law. As Paul VI states, a "right conscience" is the "true interpreter" of God's law on this question (n. 10 § 5).

One of the aspects of the question being assessed by Paul VI was that of whether spouses might use their reason to judge the demands of responsible parenthood rather than rely on biology (n. 3). This recent opinion, mentioned by the Pope, seems to offer a false dichotomy. The person, "one in body and spirit",[49] is not above his or her body, as if this were sub-personal; the body is part of the person they are. In conscience couples have to make judgments regarding their sexual behaviour as bodily human beings. The Council had called conscience the "sanctuary where man finds himself alone with God", where he recognises his moral responsibilities and is bound to follow a "correct conscience".[50] Yet, this does not mean at all that the person or couple should do this in total isolation, as if individuals or couples were free to establish what is right and wrong themselves or as if what is right (or wrong) could vary radically, or be contradictory, with everything being relative. Rather openness to God, to the teaching of the Church's Magisterium, to objective moral truth, not invented but recognised in conscience, is what is at

---

[48] Cf. Second Vatican Council, *Gaudium et spes*, n. 87; Paul VI, *Populorum progressio*, n. 37.
[49] *Gaudium et spes*, n. 14.
[50] Ibid., n. 16.

(*Respecting the Nature and the Purpose of the Marital Act*)

11. Those acts by which spouses intimately and chastely are joined together and through which human life is propagated, as the recent Council has reminded us, 'are noble and worthy'[11] and these same acts do not cease to be legitimate, even if they are foreseen to be unfruitful on the basis of causes in no way flowing from the will of the spouses, since their being ordered

---

[11] Cf. Ibid., n. 49, *A.A.S.*, LVIII (1966), p. 1070.

stake.[51] Living by that truth which accords with God's will, in respect of sexuality and marriage, as in all areas of life, is not only right, but is truly fulfilling.

With these qualifications, it remains true that it is for the spouses to assess the requirements of responsible parenthood in their concrete circumstances. Where they do so properly, evaluating the factors noted above and where they conclude sincerely that they ought not to seek to have another child for the time being or indefinitely, this judgment ought to determine their intentions, as to what they will seek to do or to avoid in relation to their conjugal acts. Their intention here to seek to avoid another child would be an upright intention of responsible parenthood (as distinct from an intention to avoid a child, made for selfish or trivial reasons). This upright intention concerns *what* they will *seek to do*; we leave aside for the moment the question of the means they may use (*how* they may seek to do this or *what* they may choose to do *in order to bring this about*). Furthermore, this upright intention would be their honest and sincere assessment of God's will for them, so that they would be bound in conscience to abide by it. As we can see, the idea that responsible parenthood is contrary to Catholic teaching is simply wrong; responsible parenthood is expressly required by Catholic teaching, expressly required in this encyclical.

11. The Pope now considers the conjugal act; he repeats the doctrine of Pius XII and of the Council, that such acts are "noble and worthy". This rejects dualistic views of the person, seeing the body and sexuality as in some way dirty or degrading, and underscores the need for an integral anthropology. It should challenge the ill-informed who think that the Catholic Church lacks or opposes such positive teaching on this matter.

The value of conjugal acts remains even if they are not fruitful in many cases. The woman's fertility is cyclical, unlike the male's; this is a way of spacing births (n. 11). A woman is infertile after the menopause, or the husband or the wife may

---

[51] Cf. John Paul II, *Veritatis splendor*, nn. 60-64.

to expressing and strengthening the union of the spouses does not cease. In fact, as is known from experience, new life does not arise from each and every conjugal union. For God has wisely disposed natural laws and times of fruitfulness such that, by these same laws and times already operating of themselves, subsequent generations are spaced at intervals. While, indeed, the Church reminds people about the precepts of the natural law which are to be observed, and which she interprets in her constant doctrine, she teaches that it is necessary that 'each and every conjugal act' (use of marriage) remain of itself open to human life being procreated.[12]

---

[12] Cf. Pius XI, Encyclical letter, *Casti Connubii, A.A.S.*, XXII (1930), p. 560; Pius XII, Allocution to Participants at the Conference of Italian Catholic Midwives, *A.A.S.*, XLIII (1951), p. 843.

be sterile for other reasons. Provided they do not deliberately cause their infertility, the conjugal act does "not cease to be legitimate", since it is still orientated to "expressing and strengthening the union of the spouses" (n. 11). This recalls the unitive meaning of the conjugal act, fostering the communion of the persons of the spouses.

Two points may be made here. First of all, the causes of infertility in the instances just listed lie beyond the control of the couple. They are not deliberate 'human acts' as such for which human beings could be held morally responsible, but they are 'acts of a man' in that they happen in the human being, without him or her willing them or bringing them about.[52] Very different is the situation where one of the spouses or both of them deliberately bring about infertility, even of particular conjugal acts. The Magisterium teaches that "each and every conjugal act ('use of marriage') must remain of itself open to human life being procreated" (n. 11). The term 'use of marriage' was a standard way in earlier moral theology of referring to the conjugal act. The significance of 'of itself' is that nothing ought to be done by either spouse to cause it to be infertile. If it is infertile for reasons beyond their control, they are not morally responsible for that, but they would be if they made an act infertile.

The text refers to 'natural law' here. Since the Magisterium is competent to teach authoritatively in matters of natural law (n. 4), we should be clear that it is not just biology which is at stake here, but moral goods and morally right or wrong behaviour. Natural moral law is the term we use to talk about the moral good or bad which can in principle be recognised even by those who do not have the benefit of divine revelation, when their moral reason is functioning correctly. Here the moral goods or meanings of marriage, expressed in the

---

[52] Cf. St Thomas Aquinas, *Summa theologiae*, I-II, q. 1, a. 1 for this key distinction in morality between an '*actus hominis*' (act of a man or of a person), which is not deliberate, such as digesting food or dreaming in sleep, and an '*actus humanus*' (human act or moral act), which is deliberately done and so can be evaluated as morally good or bad, right or wrong.

(Two Inseparable Aspects: Union and Procreation)

12. § 1 The doctrine on this matter, which has been expounded often by the Magisterium of the Church, is rooted in the indissoluble bond, established by God, which it is not allowed for the human person on his or her own initiative to break, between the unitive meaning and the procreative meaning which are both contained in the conjugal act.

§ 2 For indeed, because of its intimate character, the act of marriage, while it associates the husband and the wife in the closest bond, also makes them suitable for generating new life, according to laws inscribed in the nature itself of man and of woman. The fact is that, if each essential meaning of the same conjugal act, namely

conjugal act, meanings even non-Christians can perceive in conscience, are at stake. The text notes the fact that nature spaces births itself; where a couple with an upright intention of responsible parenthood make use of this time, the good or meaning of procreation is not being deliberately violated.

The concluding sentence of this paragraph does seem to anticipate the doctrine to be clarified, at least in respect of one of the arguments which had arisen in the Papal Commission, namely that openness to fertility be considered not in each conjugal act, but in the conjugal life as a whole (the radical new application of the older principle of totality). Each conjugal act having to be open to new life would seem to preclude this wider use of totality and would seem to preclude any contraceptive act.

12. We come now to a major development of Magisterial doctrine. In the past theologians and the Magisterium had presented doctrine on marriage in terms of St Augustine's three goods or St Thomas Aquinas' three ends of marriage. The Augustinian goods were the good of the child (procreation and education and upbringing); the good of fidelity; and the good of the sacrament (the indissoluble bond and, for two baptised Christians, later as a specific sacrament of the Church). The Thomistic ends were the primary end of the procreation and education and upbringing of children, the secondary ends of the mutual help of the spouses and that of the remedy for concupiscence (or marriage as a way of avoiding the temptation to fornication). Both had been used by the Magisterium to articulate its teaching on marriage.[53]

One problem with the Thomistic doctrine of ends was that St Thomas had understood 'ends' in a technical, philosophical way as metaphysical or part of what marriage was about in and of itself, irrespective of what people had in mind as individuals.

---

[53] Cf. St Augustine, *De bono coniugali*, nn. 1-5 in J-P. Migne, *Patrologiae latinae*, series latina prior, XL, 373-396 at 373-377; St Thomas Aquinas, *Summa theologiae*, I, q. 98, a. 1; Supplementum, q. 49, a. 2; q. 65, aa. 1, 3; Benedict XV, *Codex iuris canonici* (1917), c. 1013 § 1; Pius XI, Encyclical letter, *Casti connubii*, 30 December, 1930, 543-547, 559-561.

that of union and that of procreation, is protected, the conjugal act (use of marriage) retains entirely its meaning of mutual and true love and its ordering to the very high responsibility of parenthood to which spouses are called. We think that people of our age are well able to recognise that this doctrine is in conformity with human reason.

As long as their own ends were compatible with these essential ends and did not contradict them, there was a true marriage. However, in modern times, many people did not understand such terminology and were more likely to think of 'ends' as their own intentions. Moreover, there had been increasing calls for the Church to give some real attention to the place of love in marriage. The Second Vatican Council deliberately chose to present its doctrine on marriage in non-technical terms. It did not intend to deny or to change the earlier Magisterial doctrine on the hierarchy and subordination of ends, but it chose not to repeat it in those terms.[54] It intended to present its doctrine in a pastoral framework, in language which might be more accessible to people of our time. It certainly spoke of marriage as a community of life and love, as an irrevocable covenant, as being ordered to the good of the spouses as well as to the supreme gift of children, in a setting of conjugal love seen as mutually self-giving.[55]

Paul VI did not wish to revert to the pre-Conciliar ways of presenting doctrine on marriage; nor did he do so. We have already seen how he summarised the new Conciliar doctrine on conjugal love (n. 9). He also intentionally set his doctrine in the context of an integral anthropology. We have noticed, however, that he developed earlier, even Conciliar, doctrine by talking more explicitly about a unitive meaning of marriage and of the conjugal act, as well as the procreative meaning. The concept of 'meaning' in regard to marriage may go back to the critical work of H. Doms, writing soon after Pius XI's encyclical, where he had made a plea for love to be more fully recognised, in a book on the meaning and ends of marriage, or to D. von Hildebrand who analysed that meaning in a series of writings, culminating in a book on the essence of love.[56]

---

[54] Cf. M. Zalba, "Num concilium Vaticanum II hierarchiam finium matrimonii ignoravit, immo et transmutaverit?" in *Periodica de re morali canonica et liturgica*, 68 (1979), 613-635.

[55] Cf. Second Vatican Council, *Gaudium et spes*, nn. 47-52.

[56] Cf. H. Doms, *Du sens et de la fin du mariage*, 2ⁿᵈ edition (Desclée de Brouwer, Paris, 1937), 21-28, 68-70; original German: *Von Sinn und Zweck der Ehe* (Ostdeutsche Verlagsanstalt, Breslau, 1935); D. von Hildebrand, *Il matri-*

In this encyclical Paul VI developed doctrine by speaking of a unitive meaning of the conjugal act, as well as a procreative meaning, both being essential meanings of that act. Furthermore, he developed a new doctrinal principle, the principle of inseparability, namely that these two essential meanings of the conjugal act were linked by an "indissoluble bond" and could not be separated from one another by the human person "on his or her own initiative" (n. 12 § 1). Notice again the key distinction between what happens independently of any deliberate human action and what is wilfully brought about. To say that the unitive and procreative meanings of the conjugal act were inseparable did not mean that the act always led to procreation in fact, since we know that the act is often infertile through no intervention of the couple. Nor did it mean that they could not be separated by people acting in a certain way (that is possible); he meant that they ought never to be separated deliberately from one another.

The Pope then elaborates on the principle, which he has said is the source of the doctrine on marriage and procreation, so often taught by the Magisterium (n. 12 § 1), the principle which he is using to ground his doctrine on responsible parenthood, shortly to be outlined. The conjugal act as the most intimate act of the couple, simultaneously unites them in the deepest possible way and makes them capable of procreating children "according to laws inscribed in the nature itself of man and of woman" (n. 12 § 2). What is meant is that, through their nature of sexually differentiated human beings, the husband and wife are able to unite themselves to one another in the deepest possible way in the conjugal act, not just biologically, but in all that they are as persons (bodily, sexual, rational, spiritual beings) and in all that they are as spouses, this same act being unique because it is also the only act they could perform together in which and by which they could become cooperators

---

monio (Morcellana, Brescia, 1931): original German, *Die Ehe* (Kösel-Pustet, München, 1929): idem, *Man and Woman* (Franciscan Herald Press, Chicago, 1965); idem, *Gesammelte Werke*, III, *Das Wesen der Liebe* (Habbel, Regensburg, Kohhammer, Stuttgart, 1971).

(Fidelity to God's Plan)

13. In fact, people rightly observe that the conjugal act imposed (by one spouse) on the other spouse, having no regard for their condition nor for their just wishes, is not a true act of love, and so much so that it stands opposed to those things which the moral order rightly demands in terms of the relationship between spouses. In the same way, if they reflect on the matter, they should recognise that an act of mutual

with God in the possible transmission of new life. We see here both the unitive meaning and the procreative meaning of conjugal love and both of those meanings in the conjugal act. Not only are the two essential meanings of the conjugal act rooted in the nature of conjugal love, expressed in that act, but the principle of inseparability itself is likewise rooted in that love between husband and wife. When the conjugal act is undertaken with the principle being observed, i.e. when the unitive and procreative meanings are not separated from one another, "the conjugal act retains entirely its meaning of true love and its ordering ... to parenthood" (n. 12 § 2).

The implication of this elaboration is that, if the principle of inseparability is violated, i.e. if the two essential meanings are deliberately separated from one another, then the conjugal act loses its full meaning of uniting the couple in love and of being directed or ordered to procreation. This principle is applied implicitly to contraception in this encyclical, since that doctrine is "founded" on this "inseparable connection" (n. 12 § 1). It became important in a way that Paul VI would hardly have foreseen at the time, since it prohibits forms of procreation which arise apart from the conjugal act, where procedures and technologies, such as *in vitro* fertilisation, replace that act or substitute for it.[57]

13. Here we find a clear condemnation of forced intercourse within marriage, of a 'conjugal act' imposed on a spouse without regard for their condition or just wishes. 'Condition' refers to the spouse's health, while 'just wishes' alludes to a desire not to engage in intercourse at present for reasons which are neither unjust nor stem from unduly seeking his or her own convenience.[58] A man who comes home drunk and demands sex with his wife acts immorally, whereas her refusal would not be immoral. Such behaviour, imposed on a spouse, stands "opposed to those things which the moral order rightly

---

[57] Cf. Congregation for the Doctrine of the Faith, Instruction, *Donum vitae*, 22 February, 1987, II, B. n. 4.
[58] Cf. comments on n. 9 above.

love which may be to the detriment of the faculty of propagating life, which God, the Creator of all, has inscribed according to particular laws in that act, goes against both the divine plan according to whose norm marriage is established and against the will of the primary Author of human life. For this reason, if someone uses the gift of God, removing admittedly only in part the meaning and end of the gift itself, they go against the nature either of the man or of the woman and of their intimate relationship, and, therefore, they also set themselves up against the plan of God and of his holy will. Whoever, though, uses the gift of conjugal love, respecting the laws of generation, shows himself indeed to be not the master of the sources of life, but rather the minister of the plan established by the Creator. For just as a person does not have infinite power over his or her own body as a whole, so also and clearly, for a very special reason, they do not have such power either over their generative capacities as such, since these of their very nature are directed to the engendering of human life, whose source is God. For – our predecessor, John XXIII, recalled – 'human life is to be held by all to be a sacred reality which, from its

demands" of spouses (n. 13) and is a grave violation of the moral duties entailed in the unitive meaning of marriage. Instead of a deeper union with a spouse through an intimate act of love, there would be the sexual abuse of the person who ought to be loved more than any other in the world. At times it is thought that the Magisterium ignores such behaviour; Paul VI condemns it unequivocally.

In parallel with this the Pope also condemns any act which violates God's plan for marriage and his will as the primary author of life. Calling God the "primary Author of life" (n. 13) emphasises that the transmission of human life through procreation is not just a human act, but is one which involves the creative action of God, with whom the spouses cooperate in and through their conjugal act. Human beings cannot create other human beings, but can collaborate with God in this special act. Generally in life we distinguish primary and secondary causality. God is the primary cause of all that happens in that he renders it possible, but at the level of secondary causality human beings cause things to occur or events occur in nature and such secondary causes can be studied. God does not usually intervene directly here; even in the case of damaging natural events (such as an earthquake) or of immoral human acts (such as murders), secondary causes continue to work. By his permissive will, God allows, but does not directly will, such damage or such moral wrong.

In human procreation, such intimate acts ought to occur only between spouses and then only in a morally upright way. The creation of human life entails the creative action of God as the primary author of life, with the spouses collaborating with him. Given that the new human being has a unique dignity and that the human person has an immortal soul, making him or her capable of living with God eternally (something beyond the power of mere human beings to bring about), procreation has often been seen as entailing a more direct involvement of God's creative act, with which spouses are to collaborate through their conjugal act. In other words, human life is sacred and God is the sole master of the sources of life;

very beginning, surely requires the action of God, the Creator."[13]

(Illicit Ways of Regulating Birth)

14. § 1 Therefore, relying upon these principles of the human and Christian doctrine about marriage, we must once more proclaim to be absolutely rejected as a legitimate way of regulating the number of children the direct interruption of generation already begun and especially direct abortion, even if undertaken for a therapeutic reason.[14]

---

[13] Cf. Encyclical letter, *Mater et Magistra*, A.A.S., LIII (1961), p. 447.
[14] Cf. *The Roman Catechism of the Council of Trent*, part II, chap. VIII; Pius XI, Encyclical letter, *Casti connubii*, A.A.S., XXII (1930), pp. 562-564; Pius

spouses are to act not as masters but as "ministers of the plan of God", being at the service of life through their responsible conjugal acts and "respecting the laws of generation" in those acts (n. 13).

Applying the distinction between mastery and ministry further, we recall that, as a person does not have infinite power over his or her body as a whole, neither do they have that power over their bodily capacity to procreate. In a world where it has become common for some to claim that a woman 'has the right to do what she wants with her own body' and so directly to abort an unwanted child, described falsely as no more than 'part of her body', this key moral truth needs restating. Our bodies, including organs and faculties involved in procreation, are neither things we possess nor objects at our disposal, as if 'we' were entities apart from and above our bodies; they are part of the persons we are, share in the good of the person as such, to be respected and never manipulated. In respect of procreation, too, spouses are to act not as masters, but as ministers. This section, then, underscores the immense dignity of such conjugal acts, but it also highlights the moral responsibilities spouses have not to act against God's will either in respect of marriage in general or in respect of the transmission of human life in particular.

14. Here we come to the question of the means to be used in implementing a decision made for upright reasons to seek to avoid another child for the present or indefinitely, based on criteria examined in n. 10. Presupposing such an upright intention, there have been a number of indications as to which means are compatible with the 'moral order' or which are morally right. Thus, the choice of means may not be arbitrary, as if spouses could invent their own moral norms (n. 10 § 6). Each conjugal act is to remain open to new life (n. 11). The procreative meaning of the conjugal act is inseparably joined to its unitive meaning and is never to be severed from it deliberately (n. 12 § 1). Spouses are to act as ministers, not masters, of the sources of life in the conjugal act (n. 13).

XII, Allocution to the Italian Bio-Medical Association of St. Luke, *Discorsi e radiomessaggi di S.S. Pio* XII, pp. 191-1912; Allocution to the Participants at the Conference of Association of Italian Catholic Midwives, *A.A.S.*, XLIII (1951), pp. 842-843; Allocution to the Participants at the Conference of the Association known as 'Family Front' and to the Association of Large Families, *A.A.S.*, XLIII (1951), 857-859*; John XXIII, Encyclical letter, *Pacem in terris, A.A.S.*, LV (1963), pp. 259-260; Second Vatican Council, Pastoral Constitution, *Gaudium et spes*, n. 51, *A.A.S.*, LVIII (1966), p. 1072. (* The data given on the Vatican website in this footnote to the Latin text of Paul VI's encyclical state erroneously that the year is 1961.)

In the light of principles already examined in nn. 7-13 (n. 14 § 1), Paul VI now turns to the central questions about procreation and birth regulation, to teach as Pope the moral norms as to the means which may and which may not be used to give effect to an upright intention of responsible parenthood. The norms taught in n. 14 specify means which may not be used; these will be stated and analysed first before turning to comments he gives for not accepting arguments which had been advanced for urging a change in moral doctrine.

a. The Moral Norms Forbidding Illicit (Immoral) Practices

Even where there is an upright intention of responsible parenthood, three moral norms are taught in n. 14 which forbid:

- direct interruption of the generative process already begun, especially directly procured abortion (n. 14 § 1)

- direct sterilisation (n. 14 § 2) and

- contraception (n. 14 § 3).

i. Directly procured Abortion

The doctrine on directly procured abortion repeats constant doctrine across the centuries ("we must once more proclaim") as "to be absolutely rejected" any direct interruption once generation has begun, especially directly procured abortion. 'Procured abortion' is to be distinguished from 'spontaneous abortion', usually termed in English a 'miscarriage', provided such a miscarriage is not deliberately provoked, because, if it is, then morally it falls into the category of a procured abortion. Directly procured abortion has always been condemned by the Church; Christians were known for their opposition to this from their earliest existence in the Roman Empire where it was quite common. Then, as now, we are at odds with popular opinion. The official footnote to this paragraph shows how many recent interventions there had been on this subject by the Magisterium. In the face of laws introduced by governments pretending to allow procured abortion and of court judgments pretending to authorise direct abortions

('pretending' because what is intrinsically immoral can never be permitted or authorised), the Magisterium has since reinforced this teaching. In 1974 the Sacred Congregation for the Doctrine of the Faith condemned all directly procured abortion as intrinsically morally wrong, 'intrinsically' meaning 'of its very nature', however well-meaning the intention and however pressing the circumstances. This was repeated in the *Catechism of the Catholic Church* and in the major encyclical on human life of John Paul II, *Evangelium vitae*.[59]

There is a distinction between a directly procured abortion and an indirectly procured abortion; the former is always gravely immoral, whereas the latter can at times be morally licit, although it is not automatically so. Paul VI rightly repeats that "even if undertaken for a therapeutic reason", direct abortion remains morally wrong. Put quite simply, a good intention never justifies morally evil means. If the mother has a serious illness of the heart or the kidneys, an abortion of the child with whom she is pregnant remains a direct killing of an innocent human being, "to be respected and treated as a person from the first moment of conception", including respect for the fundamental rights of the human person, first of all the right of every innocent human being to the right to life, as more recent doctrine has further specified it.[60] Once there is conception (fertilisation), a new human being exists with these rights, so there is not a choice between mother and child, but there are two human beings, both with equal rights, to be cared for. A mother with serious cardiac or renal problems should be monitored especially throughout the pregnancy with particular care. The presumption that a direct abortion would improve her health is by no means necessarily justified, since an abortion does nothing to relieve the underlying pathology and since an abortion is a major

---

[59] Cf. Sacred Congregation for the Doctrine of the Faith, Declaration, *De abortu procurato*, 1974, nn. 8-13, 18; *The Catechism of the Catholic Church*, n. 2271; John Paul II, Encyclical letter, *Evangelium vitae*, 25 March, 1995, n. 62.

[60] Congregation for the Doctrine of the Faith, Instruction, *Donum vitae*, 22 February, 1987, Introduction, n. 4.

HUMANAE VITAE: TRANSLATION

98

intervention which is more likely to put her heart or kidneys under greater strain and may aggravate rather than alleviate the problem. Even if it would help, it would still be gravely immoral to kill the child directly and so such an action would not be justified even then.

An indirect abortion can be justified at times, but only where at issue is an action with two simultaneous effects, one good and the other bad, and where all four conditions of the principle of double effect truly apply. Thus, a woman with a cancerous uterus who is pregnant might well be urged to have a hysterectomy, legitimate under the principle of totality, to sacrifice the part of her own body for the sake of the whole, or radio- or chemo-therapy, to save her own life. Yet, such procedures would have the simultaneous effect of killing or of gravely impairing the unborn child. If all the following conditions were met, such procedures would be legitimate, but if any one of these conditions were not met, the action would be gravely morally wrong:

– The act performed must be good or indifferent, not intrinsically morally wrong. (This would often be the case; the principle of totality would make a hysterectomy legitimate were the woman not pregnant, as just explained; therapy to cure her or to prevent deterioration of her health would be legitimate in principle.)

– The intention must be only the good of saving the mother's life or health, not the abortion. The death or impairment to the child must not be intended, must remain beyond the intention. (If the mother did not want the child and was glad to be rid of him/her, to this extent the abortion would no longer be 'beyond the intention', but would be 'in the intention' or part and parcel of the intention and so she would commit a grave moral wrong.)

– The good effect (on the mother's health) must not be brought about through the evil effect, the abortion or damage to the child (precisely this would happen in any direct abortion); in other words, even where there were a morally good intention of saving the mother's life, such

§2 Equally to be condemned, as the Magisterium of the Church has several times taught, is directly to sterilise either men or women, whether permanently or only for a limited time.[15]

---

[15] Cf. Pius XI, Encyclical letter, *Casti connubii*, A.A.S., XXII (1930), p. 565; Decree of the Holy Office, dated 22 February, 1940, A.A.S., XXXII (1940), p. 73; Pius XII, Allocution to the Participants at the Conference of Association of Italian Catholic Midwives, A.A.S., XLIII (1951), pp. 843-844; Allocution to the seventh Conference of the International Association of Haematologists, A.A.S., L (1958), pp. 734-735.

a morally good end would never justify the intrinsically morally wrong means of directly and deliberately killing the unborn child.

– There must be a proportionately grave reason for performing this act because of the evil effect; in fact, there must be no other way of acting to protect the mother's life or health which would not have this evil effect, since, if there were, that would be what ought to be done and this action would be immoral. Where the pregnancy were advanced and the unborn child were at the stage of viability, an indirect abortion would not be justified, since there would not be a proportionate reason for performing it; rather, the unborn child should be delivered by Caesarian section and treated in intensive care and then the hysterectomy or other therapy should be carried out on the mother.

This centuries-old doctrine remains valid today. Direct abortion is gravely immoral, even if there are pressing reasons for judging that a couple ought to avoid another child (cf. the criteria of n. 10 above), because deliberately killing a human being is the means to that end.

ii. Direct Sterilisation

Sterilisation of a man or of a woman involves rendering that person temporarily or permanently infertile. A deliberate, direct violation of their bodily integrity, here of their fertility, would never be morally justifiable, whatever the intention or purpose behind it; any act which directly, of its nature, brought that about would be immoral.[61] Our bodies are not instruments at our disposal or sub-human products to use as we see fit, but are part and parcel of who we are as human persons (cf. n. 7 above). When we intervene on a part of the human body, we intervene on part of the person as such. We can say 'My arm hurts', or, with equal truth, 'It hurts me' or 'I am in pain'.

---

[61] Cf. Sacred Congregation for the Doctrine of the Faith, Declaration on Sterilisation, 13 March, 1975, n. 1; *The Catechism of the Catholic Church*, nn. 2297, 2399.

A direct sterilisation would mean a surgical, medical or other physical act deliberately undertaken which, of itself, would render the person sterile, seriously damaging, temporarily or permanently, their functioning as a person by rendering them unable to generate children. If the person were suffering from a pathology or disease of the genital organs which necessitated the removal of the organ or radio or chemo-therapy on the organ to prevent death or grave deterioration of health, the treatment would be justified under the principle of totality (and double effect), sacrificing the part for the sake of the whole. If such therapy were needed on another organ of the body, but that therapy would have a temporary or permanent sterilising effect, then, if all the conditions of double effect applied, the sterilisation would be the indirect effect of those procedures.

Quite different is the situation where some other purpose is invoked, where there is no actual pathology endangering the life or health of the person, but where a sterilisation is sought to avoid having more children for a serious reason (cf. n. 10), even where the mother is advised against having more children since a pregnancy might probably endanger her health or her life. Here no actual disease requires the removal or treatment impairing the functioning genital organs as such; indeed no treatment which would have a direct impact upon these organs or upon fertility is required, since whatever other health problem exists can be treated without direct impact upon such organs or fertility (e.g. medication or even surgery for a cardiac or renal condition). Even if a woman's uterus is badly damaged from earlier pregnancies and another pregnancy would be dangerous to her as well as for any child conceived, and the couple could have an upright intention of seeking to avoid a future child for this reason, since she is not pregnant, the danger is not actually present and will not become present unless she becomes pregnant. No existing pathology in her requires any intervention which would destroy or impair her fertility; any sterilisation would be a direct violation of her bodily integrity. Where a man were sterilised because of such

§ 3 To be rejected in the same way is any act whatever which may operate in such a way that procreation may be impeded. (This is so) either when conjugal intercourse is foreseen or when it is being undertaken or when it is proceeding to its natural outcomes. (It is so) whether that be the intention being sought (the end to be reached) or whether it be the means to be employed (for attaining that end).[16]

---

[16] Cf. *The Roman Catechism of the Council of Trent*, part II, chap. VIII; Pius XI, Encyclical letter, *Casti connubii*, A.A.S., XXII (1930), pp. 559-561; Pius XII, Allocution to the Participants at the Conference of Association of Italian Catholic Midwives, A.A.S., XLIII (1951), p. 843; Allocution to the seventh Conference of the International Association of Haematologists, A.A.S., L (1958), pp. 734-735; John XXIII, Encyclical letter, *Mater et Magistra*, A.A.S., LIII (1961), p. 447.

a pathology in his wife, there would be a direct mutilation of his bodily integrity, which is always gravely immoral. The good intention of responsible parenthood justifies and requires that some action be taken, but not action which is of its nature morally wrong, such as these direct sterilisations.

iii. Contraception

The specific purpose for which this encyclical was issued was to settle whether the new anovulant pill fell under the traditional condemnation of contraception in Church doctrine. Previous teachings had condemned interfering with the nature of the conjugal act so as to render it infertile. Here Paul VI states that, beyond direct abortion and direct sterilisation, contraception was also rejected as a morally upright way of regulating births.

The terms "foreseen", "when being undertaken" and "proceeding to its natural outcomes" clearly refer to something being done 'before' 'during' or 'after' the conjugal act to stop it from being fertile, even where there are good reasons to avoid another child. Clearly, the anovulant pill is included in this refusal, along with other means of contraception which might be conducted before the act (such as surgical or chemical sterilisation), those which might be employed during the act (such as condoms, diaphragms, the IUD coil or *coitus interruptus*) or those which might be used afterwards (surgical, chemical or any other form of abortion; here any form of pill which acted to destroy the unborn child, even destroying its life by preventing implantation in the womb). The doctrine stated here goes on to say that this applies whether what is done is "the intention being sought" (the end or purpose intended) or whether it is "the means to be employed" for attaining such an end. Quite simply, any and all forms of contraception are rejected, confirming the constant doctrine that had always been taught by the Church's Magisterium.

It should be noted that the text of the encyclical as such does not reject 'artificial contraception', as if there were some

§ 4 Nor indeed is it legitimate to put forward as valid those arguments which are designed to give approval to those conjugal acts which are deprived deliberately of their fruitfulness. These arguments are, namely, (1) that that evil is to be chosen which seems to be less grave or further (2) that those same (deliberately unfruitful) acts coalesce with acts which were undertaken in the past and have already been fruitful or with those which are to be undertaken in the future to form one particular act, to such an extent that they share in one and the same moral goodness of those (fruitful) acts. For indeed, the truth is that, if tolerating a moral evil which is less grave is allowed at certain times in order that some greater evil may be avoided or so that some more pressing good may be promoted,[17] it is nevertheless never allowed, not even for the gravest of reasons, to do things which are evil so that good may result from them.[18] It is never allowed, namely, to introduce into the will that which of its very nature transgresses

---

[17] Cf. Pius XII, Allocution to Participants at the fifth Conference of the Italian Association of Catholic Jurists, *A.A.S.*, XLV (1953), pp. 798-799.
[18] Cf. Rom. 3: 8.

form of 'natural contraception' which could be approved; it rejects contraception as such, all methods of contraception without exception.

b. Rejection of Arguments used to argue for a Change in Moral Norms

We have seen that a number of arguments had been put forward before the encyclical was issued, arguing that there should be a change of moral norms, at least to allow the new anovulant pill to be used when there were serious reasons for avoiding a new pregnancy (n. 3 above). Two key elements of those arguments are taken up now and are rejected, so that the norms forbidding direct abortion, direct sterilisation and contraception apply without exception. What are these two arguments?

i. The Lesser Evil Argument

Even if contraception were not to be regarded as a good as such, where it was used to avoid another pregnancy where there are serious reasons for judging that this should be avoided, it might seem "that that evil is to be chosen which seems to be less grave" (n. 14). The argument of the lesser evil has been known to Catholic moral theology for a long time, but there it is a question of tolerating a lesser evil done by another person or persons when they cannot be prevented from committing it. Before the right to religious liberty was formally taught at the Second Vatican Council (requiring respect for the erroneous consciences of those who believe in what is proposed in faiths other than the Christian faith and of those Christians who believe what is contrary to the fulness of Catholic truth), a right rooted in human nature itself, tolerating other faiths and non-Catholic Christianity had often been justified as entailing a lesser evil than the massive civil unrest or even outright wars which might otherwise be expected. An oppressive government might be tolerated as a lesser evil, compared to the major unrest and likely mass slaughter to be expected if there were an

HUMANAE VITAE: TRANSLATION

the moral order and which, as such, is judged to be unworthy of the human being, however much it may be done for the purpose that the goods of individual human beings, of families sharing the home or of human society may be defended and promoted. Therefore, a person will be completely wrong who judges that the conjugal act, deliberately deprived of its fruitfulness and, therefore, intrinsically morally wrong, can be approved as upright by being joined to those acts of intercourse which are fruitful in the conjugal life as a whole.

insurrection. There are many instances in everyday life when we tolerate the wrong other people do because changing them would not be possible or practicable in the circumstances or might provoke much greater trouble. However, the person or persons tolerating the wrong done by others are not themselves doing anything wrong as such; they do not abandon fulness of religious truth, perpetrate civil injustices caused by the government, etc. Even where others are intent on doing wrong and cannot be dissuaded, urging them to do less wrong (the lesser evil), provided this is in no way approved, can at times be justifiable. An armed robber intent on murder, who is persuaded by a customer who arrives to leave the proprietor alive, commits a grave wrong in his theft, but the customer who tolerates and even recommends that he not commit the greater wrong does no wrong himself. A politician who cannot change an abortion law, but who supports or recommends a law which would restrict the age limit within which abortions sanctioned by civil law may be conducted, provided his total opposition to abortion is known and made clear, votes for the saving of the lives which can be saved, but does no wrong, nor approves any wrong, but tolerates a continuing wrong he or she is not in a position to prevent.[62]

The argument that contraception might be a 'lesser evil' than the unwanted consequences of another pregnancy is not at all the argument of lesser evil known to Catholic moral theology; it would not be a case of tolerating the wrong of contraception done by others, but of deliberately doing that wrong themselves as a couple and, probably, on a systematic or regular basis. As Paul VI puts it: "... the truth is that, if tolerating a moral evil which is less grave is allowed at certain times in order that some greater evil may be avoided or so that some more pressing good may be promoted, it is nevertheless never allowed, not even for the gravest of reasons, to do things which are

---

[62] Cf. John Paul II, *Evangelium vitae*, n. 74.

evil so that good may result from them". Put very simply, a morally good end or intention of avoiding another child for serious reason never justifies the moral wrong of contraception. In the case considered here, it would mean not tolerating someone else's moral wrong-doing, but the couple themselves actually intending that wrong, "to introduce into the will that which of its very nature transgresses the moral order and which is to be judged unworthy in the human being" and actually themselves doing that wrong. This is so whatever the good intention, "however much it may be done for the purpose that the goods of individual human beings, of families sharing the home or human society may be defended and promoted" (n. 14); the morally good end or intention does not justify the morally wrong means.

ii. The Revised Principle of Totality

We have seen that it had been proposed that contraception might be justified in some instances on the basis of the "so-called principle of totality" (n. 3). The principle of totality as such justifies, for example, amputating a gangrenous limb to save a person's life, sacrificing the part for the sake of the whole or the total – hence the name 'totality'. However, in regard to responsible parenthood, the same principle was being invoked by name, whereas what was being proposed under cover of that name was something very different. The suggestion was that the conjugal acts of the 'whole' or 'totality' of the life of the couple should be taken together as one and that the moral quality of their conjugal acts should be judged not one by one, but together over the whole of their married life. Thus, if they had already had children in their married life to date or if they were intending to have children in their married life in the future, then their married lives as a whole should be judged to have been or to be fruitful or open to procreation and any contracepted acts undertaken at present or for some time should not be judged as morally wrong, but, on the

basis of these prior or future acts or both, as morally legitimate. This proposal would have given a radically different content to the principle of totality and would have been a very different principle indeed; hence it is referred to in this encyclical as the "so-called principle of totality".

Paul VI uses the argument he had used against the lesser evil or lesser wrong against this revised principle of totality too. Precisely, it is never allowed to do what is morally wrong, even for a good intention. If this radically different version of totality were employed, it would mean that every time a couple contracepted the contracepted act would be rendered 'good' in some way because of previous or future good conjugal acts. Perhaps, we can illustrate this argument with other examples. Someone under severe financial pressures in the family over a difficult period of time who made false declarations on tax-return forms in that period could hardly claim properly that such acts were good, just or licit because previously and subsequently they had always told the full truth to the tax authorities. A young person of good character, whose widowed mother were in serious difficulties at a given time, who 'took things from work' to supplement his meagre income and help her out might have a good intention and might be acting under pressure of circumstances, but what he did would not be 'good ' or 'right'. That he 'had never done it in the past', 'would never do it again' and 'over the totality of his life he had acted justly', would not render his current acts of theft 'just'.

Paul VI's rejection of the lesser evil argument and of the new version of totality in regard to contraception reflects the Biblical and universal moral truth that a good end, purpose or intention never justifies morally wrong means. As well as our intentions, the morality of what we do stems from the moral object of the act; what we deliberately choose to do to put that intention into effect necessarily qualifies

(Licitness of Therapeutic Means)

15. However, the Church does not consider at all illicit those acts of therapy which are necessary for the curing of sicknesses of the body, even if an impediment to procreation may arise from them and even if this is foreseen, provided that this impediment, no matter what the reason, is not directly intended.[19]

---

[19] Cf. Pius XII, Allocution to Participants at the 26th Conference of the Italian Society of Urologists, *A.A.S.* XLV (1953), pp. 674-675; Allocution to the seventh Conference of the International Association of Haematologists, *A.A.S.* L (1958), pp. 734-735.

our individual acts as morally good or bad, morally right or wrong, and also affects the persons we are and the persons we become.[63] What we do deliberately makes us thieves or fraudsters or just citizens, married couples who respect their fertility and the gift of life from God or who act against these goods of marriage.

Paul VI rejected bad arguments for contraception. We shall look at arguments which may support his doctrine in our general remarks in the Appendix to this commentary.

15. This paragraph states that the Church does not consider immoral those acts of therapy "necessary for the curing of sicknesses of the body", even if a contraceptive effect results from such acts, even if this is foreseen.

This sounds rather strange, coming after the clear rejection of all contraception in n. 14. Yet, it involves two principles we have seen already. First of all, an amputation or mutilation might be needed to save the person's life; a vasectomy or a hysterectomy performed because of a cancerous tumour would be "necessary for the curing of the sickness of the body" and would be justified under the classical principle of totality, sacrificing the part for the sake of the whole.

Another possibility envisaged here would be a medical or surgical procedure "necessary for curing the sickness of the body" of the person, where the simultaneous effect of the medicine or surgery required was sterilising or contraceptive. Radio-therapy in the area of the genital organs or chemo-therapy for any cancerous tumour might have such effects either on a temporary or even on a permanent basis.

In both of these instances the principles of double effect, and/or of totality are at issue. In other words, the therapeutic principle of acting to heal, alleviate or prevent serious illness, can involve applying either or both of those principles.[64] Unlike

---

[63] Cf. John Paul II, *Veritatis splendor*, nn. 78-79.
[64] Cf. L. Gormally, "Medicine as a Profession and the Meaning of Health as its Goal" in L. Gormally (ed.), *Issues for a Catholic Bioethic: Proceedings of the International Conference for the celebration of the Twentieth Anniversary*

the indirect abortion considered above, here the question is of an action which prevents the conception of a new human being through the fertilisation of the ovum by sperm.

Where surgery or other therapy were contemplated which might or would have a sterilising or contraceptive impact, the principle of totality would legitimate what was needed to save life or prevent a grave deterioration of health. With the principle of double effect, the four conditions would need to be checked. If all four truly apply, then the action is morally upright, as n. 15 indicates; if any one of them does not properly apply, the act is immoral. Thus, an actual, additional intention, to use the surgery or other therapy to function as a contraceptive to block the conception of a child would mean that the bad effect had become part of the intention and so would be morally wrong on that account. Where only the good effect were intended and where it would not come through the bad effect, where any healing would be the effect of the surgery or other therapy and not of the sterilising or contraceptive effect of such intervention, provided there were a proportionately serious reason for taking this act with two simultaneous effects, such intervention to prevent death or cure or prevent serious illness would be legitimate.

The norm given here, then, does not contradict what has just been said, but specifies it further in a consistent way. One situation often thought to be covered by this norm is that of regularising a woman's very disturbed and problematic menstrual cycle, perhaps a chronic condition, perhaps more acute. This would certainly be covered by this norm in principle. However, if this were to be undertaken through the administration of the anovulant or contraceptive pill, it would presuppose that this exercised a truly contraceptive, and not an abortifacient, action. The pill on the markets forty years

of the Foundation of the Linacre Centre (The Linacre Centre, London, 1999), 173-183 at 179-180; E. Sgreccia e M-L. Di Pietro, "La persona e il modello personalista" in E. Sgreccia, A.G. Spagnolo, e M-L. Di Pietro (a cura di), *Bioetica: Manuale per i diplomi universitari della sanità* (Vita e pensiero, Milano, 2002), 149-167 at 163-164.

ago had a high oestrogen content and did function mainly as a contraceptive, blocking ovulation. Given the problems of side-effects on the woman's future fertility and risks of cancer from persistent usage, a lower oestrogen pill with a higher progesterone content has been more usual in recent years, to the point where pills of this kind are the only ones normally available. The problem is that these pills act either predominantly or as a back-up as abortifacient pills; they act upon the endometrium or lining of the womb to stop it from preparing itself to receive the newly conceived unborn human being, preventing implantation.[65] The recent attempt to re-define conception as occurring only at implantation, to talk of a pre-embryo as distinct from the embryo and to speak of procured abortion as occurring only where the embryo or foetus is destroyed after implantation, is a misuse and a distortion of language and hence an abuse and a distortion of the truth of what is involved. The practical difficulty is that, in the cases at issue here, where a truly contraceptive but not abortifacient pill might be legitimately used for strictly therapeutic purposes as explained, a pill which was essentially abortifacient could not be so used, since it would destroy the entirely innocent, newly conceived human being.

Although this paragraph only deals with therapeutic actions and, in the case of double effect, envisages using procedures with only an indirectly contraceptive effect, an indirectly contraceptive effect of another action could be legitimate where the two effects of the one (otherwise legitimate) action were simultaneous. The instance of legitimate self-defence against foreseen rape is a case in point; where soldiers have been systematically raping women as they take over villages or areas, the use of a contraceptive (but not abortifacient) pill would be justified along the lines just explained, the sperm being the extension of the unjust aggression. This would not apply once conception had

---

[65] Cf. M-L. Di Pietro, "L'educazione alla sessualità e la procreazione responsabile" in E. Sgreccia, A.G. Spagnolo, e M-L. Di Pietro (a cura di), *Bioetica: Manuale per i diplomi universitari della sanità*, 313-338 at 331-334.

(*Licitness of Recourse to Infertile Periods*)

16. § 1 On the other hand, against the doctrine of the Church on this matter of living out the morals of marriage, some people in our times, as we have indicated above (n. 3), put forward the claim that human reason has the right and the responsibility to moderate those forces which irrational nature brings before it and to direct them to that end which is to be followed which corresponds to the good of the person. Now, in regard to the matter under discussion, several people ask: surely it must be appropriate in so many circumstances that reason limit the generation of children by artificial methods, if, acting in this way, better provision may be made for the peace and harmony of the family,

occurred, since then the newly conceived human being, entirely innocent of any aggression and completely incapable of such aggression, would be the direct victim of what would be an abortifacient procedure. It is even more delicate where rape has occurred. If ovulation has not taken place, a pill can operate as a true contraceptive, but thereafter it functions as an abortifacient; the time taken diagnosing ovulation and upright moral judgments are less likely to be observed than taking any pill regardless of the real probability of an abortifacient rather than a contraceptive action.

Very recently, there has been a question raised as to whether this paragraph of Paul VI's encyclical might make it morally permissible to use a condom where a husband and wife wanted to express their love for one another through the conjugal act and avoid any danger of adultery by refusing such an expression of their love, where one of them was HIV positive. This controversial question is examined separately in more general reflections on the encyclical at the end of this book.

16. A couple's judgment that they ought to avoid another child at present (n. 10) cannot justify using contraception (n. 14). While approving the use of reason, which marks us out from animals and from blind instinct (n. 16 § 1), respect for the moral "order established by God", where a (morally good) end does not justify the (morally wrong) means, is still required.

Such couples may "follow the natural cycles immanent in the faculties of generating new life" (n. 16 § 2), in other words the cycles of fertility and infertility which are found in the woman. Engaging in the conjugal act when it is judged that the wife is in the infertile phase of her cycle, the couple "legitimately make use of a faculty given ... by nature", as opposed to contraception where they "impede the same faculty" (n. 16 § 3). This complex language means that, although they may have the same justifiable and morally upright intention of seeking to avoid a child, using the infertile time of the

and more suitable conditions for educating and raising the children who already have been born may be assured. To this question it is necessary to give a clear response. Certainly, the Church before all others is the first in praising and in commending the use of the human intellect in action which associates the human person, distinguished by reason, so effectively with their Creator. But she affirms that this is to be undertaken in such a way that the order of things established by God is respected.

§ 2 If, therefore, there may be just causes for spacing subsequent generations of children, which arise from the conditions of the body or the mind of the spouses or from external circumstances, the Church teaches that it is then licit for spouses to follow the natural cycles, immanent in the faculties of generating new life, having conjugal intercourse in those times which, as far as can be told, may be infertile (lacking in conception) and for them to regulate the birth of children in such a way that the doctrine about morals which we have just expounded is in no way violated.[20]

§ 3 The Church is coherent with herself and with her doctrine when she judges that spouses are allowed to make use of infertile periods and when

---

[20] Cf. Pius XII, Allocution to the Participants at the Conference of Association of Italian Catholic Midwives, A.A.S., XLIII (1951), p. 846.

cycle involves the couple acting in a way which tries to avoid conception, whereas contraception is acting directly to try to prevent a new child being conceived by doing something before, during or after the conjugal act to try to block or disable its potentially procreative action. The non-contracepting couple abstain from the conjugal act during the fertile phase of the cycle, doing nothing to stop the act giving rise to new life by what they actually do before, during or after the act and they give witness to their love in and through that conjugal act. Contracepting couples choose not to avoid the conjugal act during the fertile period, but deliberately interfere with it as described.

The Magisterium does not lay down any particular method or methods of natural regulation of birth; any such methods may be used, provided that there are serious reasons for limiting births (n. 10). If the reasons are not serious, but trivial or selfish, or if there is an anti-life mentality, using natural methods does not make the act morally upright; it is immoral by reason of their immoral intention. A couple with good reasons to avoid pregnancy, though, may use whichever natural method suits them best.

The 'rhythm method', discovered by Ogino and Knaus independently in the late 1920s and early 1930s was a major discovery of the fertile and infertile cycles in the woman. The 'temperature method' of gauging the basal body temperature of the woman, discovered in the middle of the last century, enabled women to discern the time of ovulation through the rise in the basal (basic) body temperature. The Billings method or ovulation method discovered in 1971 involves assessing the type of cervical mucus, with moist, clear mucus signalling fertility and thick, opaque mucus infertility. The symptom-thermal method involves using a series of indicators of fertility and infertility. New research suggests that more accurate indicators may be found (e.g. computerised thermometers, monitoring the ovaries, etc.)[66], research the Magisterium has encouraged in this very encyclical (n. 24) in the interests of

---

[66] Cf. M-L. Di Pietro, "L'educazione alla sessualità ...", loc. cit., 331.

she reproves as always illicit the use of those things which directly work against conception, even if this second way of acting seeks to base itself on arguments of the former which appear to be upright and serious. Yet, these two situations differ from one another completely; in the former instance, the spouses legitimately make use of a faculty given to them by nature; in the other case, in fact, they impede the same faculty, so that the order of generation may not continue its natural processes. If it is not to be denied that the spouses in both cases by mutual and certain consent wish to avoid a child for sound (probable) reasons, and that they have it as their firm conviction that no children will be born, nevertheless, it is equally the case that, in the first instance only, this is done in such a way that the spouses themselves are strong enough to abstain from the marital act in times conducive to fruitfulness as often as the procreation of children may not be desired for just reasons; when, however, times not suitable for conception return, they act in such a way that they make use of intercourse to give witness to their mutual love and to protect the fidelity they have promised to one another. These same spouses, acting in this way (doing these things), clearly, truly and surely provide witness of authentic (right) love.

establishing ever more reliable, morally upright means for couples with a proper, upright intention to avoid another pregnancy, to be able to do so.

If *Humanae vitae* approves 'natural' methods, but rejects 'artificial' methods, of regulating birth, it does not approve of natural methods just because they are natural, nor does it reject artificial methods just because they are artificial. Where the intention is upright, it approves of means of avoiding another conception (identifying the fertile/ infertile phase and then acting accordingly by avoiding the conjugal act in the fertile time and resuming this way of expressing love and of fostering fidelity (n. 16 § 3) in the infertile time), while rejecting all behaviour which seeks to block or prevent the conjugal act from being procreative. This key difference between behaviour which is contraceptive and behaviour which is not is considered more deeply in our further reflections.

(*Grave Consequences of Ways of Regulating Birth Artificially*)

17. § 1 Upright people can also be persuaded more fully of the truth of the doctrine which the Church proposes in this matter, if they turn their minds to those things which will come about from the means adopted and the grounds put forward for restricting artificially the increase of births. In the first place they themselves may recognise what a wide and easy road can be opened by this way of acting both to conjugal infidelity and to the general weakening of the discipline of morals. Nor is long experience necessary for someone to discover human infirmity and to understand that people – and especially the young, so subject to the pressure of their desires – stand in need of incitements to observe the moral law and that it is wrong to proffer to them the easy road to violating the law itself. It is indeed to be feared that husbands, already accustomed to these ways of blocking conception, may forget the reverence due to their wives and, putting the well-being of their bodies and minds in second place, may make their wives into instruments at the service of their own desire and no longer value them as companions with whom they ought to

17. Here there is an attempt to look at the question of responsible parenthood from the perspective of the consequences that would be likely to arise as a result of adopting a contraceptive solution to the question being examined. Such an approach might persuade "upright people more fully of the truth" of Church doctrine on the means being adopted or about the arguments people use to try to justify them (n. 17 § 1). Consequentialism (that something is good or bad, right or wrong, on the basis of the consequences it is likely to produce) can indicate right and wrong in some limited instances, but cannot provide a proper basis for moral judgments as a whole; in this latter sense it was rejected by Paul VI (n. 14) and it has since been strongly condemned by John Paul II.[67] Yet, at times people may be persuaded more easily that something is right or wrong if they see what consequences actually arise from it. Paul VI's remarks here have been prophetic; some people may find his teaching easier to accept and to follow on such a basis.

Paul VI saw the following as likely consequences of contraception:

– It may open the way easily to infidelity between spouses.

– It may gradually weaken the discipline of morals. This is not specified, but may mean people engaging in contraception are more likely to engage in other sexual acts or in acts against human life or simply that their sense of right and wrong in general may be undermined.

– All of us, but especially the young, need help to do what is right, especially when it requires discipline on our part, as for example, with chastity; providing ways which may seem to allow people to escape from the responsibilities of their behaviour could weaken sexual morality and

---

[67] Cf. John Paul II, *Veritatis splendor*, nn. 74-75.

go through life with respect and with love.

§ 2 Next, careful consideration is to be given to what a dangerous power is granted in this way to those members of government, who are not at all attentive to the precepts of the moral law. Surely no-one could criticise the highest authorities of the state in trying to resolve the difficulties of the whole of their nation, if they were to adopt that which were recognised as legitimate for spouses in resolving a problem in a particular family? Who could prevent public authorities from employing methods against conceiving children which they judge to be the more efficacious, even from ordering them to be adopted by everyone, as often as they consider it necessary? In this way, clearly, it may happen that people, when they wish to avoid the difficulties they find in (observing) the divine law, which they may experience as individuals, as families or living in society, may concede power to the decision of public authority to interfere in what is above all a responsibility of the spouses, proper and intimate to them as such.

§ 3 For this reason, unless we wish the duty of procreating life to be left to the arbitrary

morality in general, especially in the young.

– Husbands may start to regard and to treat their wives as objects of sexual pleasure, rather than as human beings to be respected as such, even and especially in the intimacy of the conjugal act. Here there seems to be in mind that, if the husband knows that the wife is taking contraceptives or presses her to take such measures, he is likely to be less restrained in his sexual demands, insisting upon sex whenever he wants it, with the pretext that a child can be prevented by her contracepting, regardless of her state of health, of their precarious situation, or of her just wishes or needs.

– Beyond the couple and the family, governments are likely to use policies of contraception, promoting it, supporting it or even imposing it in an utterly unjust intrusion into responsibilities which it is for the couple to judge (n. 10). This very real danger and reality, which Paul VI had already condemned the year before, made the doctrine of the encyclical very welcome in countries like the Philippines as a protection against unjust State interference. According to the principle of subsidiarity, a greater body, such as the State, should not intervene in what individuals, families or smaller intermediate groups can do properly themselves. As the Pope states, it is "above all a responsibility of the spouses, proper and intimate to them" (n. 17 § 2), to judge whether or not they should seek another child (n. 10), although this does not mean that they may employ any means they wish (n. 14).

Arguing from consequences which may arise from an act and judging the morality of what we do on that basis is a faulty and inadequate approach to morality. We cannot always know what the consequences will be, what we foresee may not happen, we tend to think of immediate consequences and neglect or be ignorant of longer-term but perhaps more dramatic consequences. Thus, a wife who used the pill for good motives and thought that all she was doing was 'behaving responsibly'

decision of human beings, we must necessarily recognise that there are some limits beyond which it is not licit to proceed in the power which a person can exercise over his or her own body in undertaking tasks which are natural to it; limits, we say, which it is licit for no-one, either as a private individual or as one endowed with public authority, to violate. These limits are not established for any other reason than that of the reverence which is due to the human body as a whole and to its natural functions, according to the principles which we have recalled above and to the right understanding of the so-called principle of totality, which our predecessor, Pius XII, clarified.[21]

---

[21] Cf. Pius XII, Allocution to Participants at the 26th Conference of the Italian Society of Urologists, *A.A.S.* XLV (1953), pp. 674-675; Allocution to the Leaders and Members of the Italian Society of 'cornea' Transplants and of the Italian Union of the Blind, *A.A.S.* XLVIII (1956), pp. 461-462.

as people put it, might face consequences unforeseen and unwanted by her and perhaps also by her husband, if he came to respect her less, had intercourse when he wanted and so came to pay her less regard and take her for granted; instead of nurturing their love, it might weaken to the point where, out of boredom and the bad habits of thinking and acting which had become part of his life, he went with someone else, ruining their marriage.

One aspect of Paul VI's concerns was how people might consider and treat their bodies (n. 17 § 3). Recalling the Second Vatican Council's teaching that the human being on earth is "one in body and spirit" ('*corpore et anima unus*'); the body is not some *thing* which we have or possess to do with as we please, but is part of the *person*. We have "power" over our bodies in the sense that we can cause them to act in a particular way, to walk, talk, write, etc., but it is always gravely morally wrong to treat one's own body or the bodies of others as objects. This is why the Pope insists that there are moral limits which ought never to be violated, out of the "reverence due to the human body as a whole and to its natural functions, according to the principles ... recalled above and to the right interpretation of the principle of totality" (n. 17 § 3). Neither on our own authority, nor on the authority of the state, may we violate that dignity through our bodily actions.

When the Pope speaks of the powers we have over our bodies, in the context of this encyclical, he clearly has in mind the sexual drive, urge, tendency or capacity, by which human beings are capable of expressing love to one another and of generating new life in cooperation with God (nn. 8, 11-12). Maybe some of the consequences which he outlined in this section may help us to see that there are moral limits to what ought to be done in respect of sexual behaviour. We are not like animals which function on the basis of mere sexual instinct; we can think because of our reason and understand the meaning of the human body, the dignity of the person to be protected in all our dealings with one another and especially to be honoured and respected by married couples in their intimate, sexual lives. Even

(The Church, Guarantor of Authentic Human Values)

18. § 1 It can be foreseen that perhaps not everyone may be able easily to accept a doctrine of this kind which has been transmitted, since too many voices are raised, spread by the more recent instruments of communication, which are in disagreement with the Church. However, it is not to be wondered at that the Church is placed alongside her divine Founder as 'a sign of contradiction'.[22] Nor for that reason does she lay aside the office enjoined upon her of preaching humbly and firmly the whole moral law, whether natural law or the law of the Gospel.

§ 2 Since the Church did not establish this two-fold law, she cannot be its arbiter, but only its guardian and interpreter. She can never be allowed to declare licit what is truly immoral, since that of its very nature always stands opposed to the real good of the person.

---

[22] Cf. Lk. 2: 34.

those who do not understand all the Pope says in this encyclical or who find it hard to live by can grasp the importance of this point. Even if there are serious reasons for a couple to seek to avoid another pregnancy, what they deliberately do to put that intention into effect can be morally good or morally bad, depending upon how they use and treat one another as persons, in their bodily and sexual behaviour and in their attitude to any new child conceived through their intimate acts.

18. In concluding the more directly doctrinal section of the encyclical, Paul VI acknowledges that many people may not find the teaching easy to accept, especially given the attention and discussion of the question in the mass media. He makes two important observations: the first is that the Church's Magisterium has to teach what is true, not what is popular; the second is that the Church is not at all opposed to progress, but is concerned that any progress be authentically human, developed in a morally upright way and put to morally good use. We shall look at these in turn.

a. The Magisterium's Duty to Teach the Truth

– The Church's Magisterium cannot refuse to teach this or any other doctrine just because it is unpopular or is challenged by others.

– Like Jesus, the Church needs to be a "sign of contradiction", in other words, not to be afraid to stand out against the opinions and practices of others, of many or even of the majority.

– The Church's Magisterium has not invented or made up this doctrine or teaching. Rather, she "cannot be its arbiter, but only its guardian and interpreter" (n. 18 § 1). The reference at this point to a "two-fold law" indicates that the doctrine is found rooted in divine revelation, but also that its truth is capable of being recognised even by those who do not know or accept Christian revelation when their reason is functioning correctly (natural moral law).

§ 3 While she guards the moral law on marriage in its fulness, the Church knows for sure that she is making a contribution to the task of establishing a true culture of civilisation among human beings. Moreover, she encourages them not to abdicate their (properly moral) duties by handing themselves over to (mere) technological systems. She does this so that she may safeguard the dignity of the spouses. Acting for this reason and adhering to the example and to the doctrine of her divine Saviour, the Church shows herself as accompanying with sincere and generous love people whom she strives to help on this earthly pilgrimage 'not for any other reason than that they may share as sons (and daughters) the life of the living God, of the Father of all'.[23]

---

[23] Cf. Paul VI, Encyclical letter, *Populorum progressio*, A.A.S., LIX (1967), p. 268.

– The Church's Magisterium cannot teach what is untrue; nor can it declare something to be right which is morally wrong, which can only damage the human being.

b. The Church's Approach to Technology and to Development

The teaching in this encyclical is presented as the Church contributing to a "true culture of civilisation" (n. 18 § 2), encouraging people, out of a love which accompanies them through life, to keep to their "properly moral duties". This implies "not abandoning themselves to (mere) technological systems" (n. 18 § 2).[68]

This statement can be and has been misunderstood and mis-interpreted. It has sometimes been said that the Church is opposed to science and technology, having in mind here that science and technology have enabled human beings to discover a great deal about how human procreation functions at the biological level and to learn how to intervene to stop conception. If people want to contracept for selfish reasons or to accompany immoral sexual behaviour outside of marriage, many would have said then that they were wrong, even morally wrong, but people ask why should married couples with good reason to space births not make use of these new technologies?

The idea that the Church is opposed to science and technology is simply false. The gifts of reason, the understanding of nature, the discovery of what can help the human person to live better individually and in society is to be welcomed. We recall the doctrine of the 'hierarchy of values', that people are more important than things, which can however be useful, that 'progress' or 'development' is not just a matter of amassing more and more things.[69] Who a person is, is more important than what a person has. Some inventions or discoveries

---

[68] I have added the word 'mere' in the translation to bring out better the point the Pope is making.
[69] Cf. *Gaudium et spes*, n. 35.

III

(Pastoral Directives)

(The Church, Mother and Teacher)

19. However, these words of ours will hardly express the thoughts and concerns of the Church, Mother and Teacher of all the nations, in a clear enough manner unless, having first instructed people about the law of God on marriage which is to be safeguarded and implemented, they also sustain them in regulating the number of children in an upright way in the midst of very difficult conditions of life to which the families and nations in our time are subjected. For the Church cannot conduct herself towards people in a way other than that of our divine Redeemer; thus, she recognises their weakness, has compassion on the crowds and receives sinners. Yet,

are put to very immoral uses, such as using nuclear power to destroy others instead of to help them, such as manipulating in a possessive way what is discovered or produced to deprive others of access to them in an unjust way. This is not a rejection of science and technology, but a critical assessment of what they do, on the basis of this moral principle of the hierarchy of values. This doctrine, taught strongly by Paul VI himself in a major encyclical on social justice in 1967, has been repeated and strengthened by John Paul II.[70] The key implication is that the development of contraceptive technologies means we have more techniques available, but that their use would not be conducive to true human development or to authentic married love. The Magisterium, even if unpopular, can only proclaim this truth about what is good and fulfilling in marriage and in conjugal love.

19. The pastoral section of the encyclical opens with a reflection on the role of the Magisterium, combining the truth of God's law on marriage and the family with pastoral concern for the difficulties people face in living this out in their marital and familial lives. It is often thought that the Magisterium should show pastoral sensitivity or understanding for people in difficulty, but there is no real pastoral sensitivity which is not based upon truth. This combined approach was that of Jesus; so the Pope could not do other than repeat "the law which of its very nature is proper to human life" in its "basic truth", a moral and not just a biological law, "with the assistance of the Spirit of God".

Pastoral help and guidance cannot be divorced from moral truth; much less can they be opposed to it. Telling people to use contraceptives, contrary to Church teaching, is wrong, even if it may be popular. It leads people in the wrong direction or mis-guides them. It cannot even be right as an imagined temporary expedient (use contraceptives 'in your situation',

---

[70] Paul VI, *Populorum progressio*, nn. 20-22; John Paul II, *Sollicitudo rei socialis*, n. 15.

she cannot do other than teach the law which of its very nature is proper to human life, restored to its basic truth, with the assistance of the Spirit of God.[24]

(The Possibility of Observing Divine Law)

20. The doctrine of the Church, which promulgates the divine law itself, about ordering rightly the increasing number of children undoubtedly will seem to many to be such that it can be observed only with great difficulty, indeed even that it is completely impossible to observe it. Yet, in truth, just as with all goods which are

---

[24] Cf. Rom. 8.

'for the time being'), since what is of its nature wrong cannot be made right by circumstances.

Although we often make progress haltingly and with reverses (gradually), it is necessary to distinguish between gradual progress with sustained commitment to what is right and good and reverses, which, as such, cannot be good, even if we learn from them. In its pastoral care, the Church always supports those who struggle to do right, even if progress is slow (the law of graduality), but it denies that what is wrong can be good, legitimate or permissible, reducing the demands of moral truth because the truth as such is thought to be too unpalatable. Such a misguided pastoral approach (the graduality of the law) would damage the very people the Church ought to be supporting and sustaining. This distinction between these two radically different approaches, signalled by Paul VI, was reinforced by Pope John Paul II, who condemned the graduality of the law, but fully endorsed the law of graduality.[71]

To say that the Church "cannot do other than teach" the moral truth on responsible parenthood, taught "with the assistance of the Spirit of God", reminds us that the Magisterium does not invent, devise or decide what moral truth should be. Paul VI does not offer a mere personal opinion; he proclaims what is true about marriage and the transmission of life.

20. Here it is acknowledged that the doctrine of the encyclical, rejecting directly procured abortion, direct sterilisation and contraception as legitimate ways of regulating births, even where there are good reasons for seeking to avoid a child, may appear hard or even impossible to live out. The general point is made that we often have to strive long and hard to achieve anything worthwhile. We may consider students struggling for years to learn, people working long hours, in dangerous, unpleasant or exhausting jobs and careers, parents striving over years to bring up their children as well as they can, etc.

---

[71] Cf. John Paul II, Apostolic Exhortation, *Familiaris consortio*, 22 November, 1981, nn. 9, 34.

outstanding in nobility and usefulness, this law requires firm intentions and much effort from individuals, from families and from the human community. Indeed, it cannot be observed without the helping grace of God, by which the good will of human beings is supported and strengthened. For those, however, who diligently reflect on the matter, those efforts will be seen actually to increase the dignity of the person and to confer benefits on human society.

All of this requires sustained effort, but that is based on "firm intentions" to do good, renewed and pursued perseveringly. Our intentions and effort to do what is good and to avoid wrong are aided by God's grace or life within us, if we are Christians (with the specific sacramental grace of matrimony for two baptised spouses), but God works in a way known only to him to sustain other people too in what is right and good, also in their married lives.

It can be difficult at times to do what is right, if we risk being unpopular or if it is something demanding, even where it is an isolated or occasional matter. Yet, to live in a morally good way is not impossible. Virtue arises when we commit ourselves intentionally to some true good (here the goods of love of wife and husband, of parents and children, the good of new life to be welcomed and nurtured) and to putting it into practice systematically, with "firm and persevering determination".[72] In lives spent trying to develop virtues such as truthfulness, justice, honesty, respect for life, fidelity, we are not yet perfect and we need continually to combat pressures from our own personal weaknesses and failures, from others in society, and from our circumstances, to abandon the good and to do wrong. More positively, perseverance in good intentions and in living practically by these goods is essential if we are be virtuous, do good, and foster good in others. God's life in Christ's disciples is a powerful, interior reality which heals and sustains us always in this endeavour.

With regard to the theme of this encyclical, the goods at stake are those of life-long, marital fidelity, mutual self-giving love between the spouses, children and their upbringing. Whatever pressing circumstances may justify a judgment of conscience that a couple ought to try to avoid another pregnancy, children as such are never to be thought of as a 'disease' against which to be innoculated, a 'problem' or a 'nuisance' to be attacked or destroyed. Innocent human life is never to be considered as other than to be welcomed

---

[72] John Paul II, Encylical letter, *Sollicitudo rei socialis*, n. 38 – on the virtue of solidarity in (international) social justice.

(Self-Control)

21. The correct and morally upright regulation of the birth of children, however, requires first from the spouses that they recognise and value fully the true goods of life and of the family and similarly that they become accustomed to controlling themselves and their passions perfectly. There is really no doubt that there is a need for self-denial to command the urges of nature, by the

and cherished. A child is never to be reduced to a 'product', evaluated, accepted or rejected according to criteria of what others desire or prefer. An 'anti-life mentality' is incompatible with any pursuit of virtue. Fostering attitudes and commitments in conscience to these aspects of the fundamental good of the person, of life (born or unborn), of the good of the child, is a serious moral obligation for all.

Chastity, the key virtue for responsible parenthood, is not a repression of our sexuality, but is the positive living out of our relationships as sexual human beings, by which we never degrade ourselves or others as objects of sexual gratification, but always cherish the human body in its sexual dimension as part of the person. Sexuality and the sexual inclination between man and woman (Gen. 1: 26-27) are part of God's blessing and gift in creating human beings, a good which remains, despite the damage done by sin. Chastity means recognising, welcoming and directing this gift in our lives as sexual human beings in a way which integrates it into truly human acts and behaviour, uniquely important in the conjugal relationship and in the conjugal act. A real intention in conscience, a firm and persevering determination to pursue these goods and to avoid their opposites, in the face of pressure to do otherwise, is both possible and necessary. Virtuous living in marriage is possible and is a source of happiness for the couple and for the family, as so many have found.

21. The virtue of chastity is specifically considered, in relation to responsible parenthood in general, which is not just a question of 'methods'. The Pope stresses the need for an appreciation of the key goods to which this question relates, those of life and of the family, goods often taken for granted in the debates of 40 years ago. The massive extension of abortion, 'alternative models of family' (comprising deliberately sought single-parent families, homosexual 'families'), and even attempts to forbid the use of 'father' and 'mother' (replacing them with 'parent'), make Paul VI's remarks especially apposite and prophetic.

operation of reason and of free will, so that the meanings of love proper to the conjugal life may be in harmony with the right (moral) order, which is required especially for the practice of continence to be observed at particular intervals of time. Indeed, a discipline of this sort, from which the purity of the spouses shines forth, certainly is not opposed to their love for one another, but fills that same love with greater human meaning. If a discipline of this kind demands a constant intention of effort, yet the spouses fully ennoble themselves in its saving virtue and are endowed with spiritual goods. For it brings to the community of the home the many fruits of tranquillity and peace and helps to resolve difficulties of other kinds. It fosters the care and protection of one spouse towards the other. It helps the spouses to put aside what is unduly selfish, which is opposed to authentic charity, and it builds up in them an awareness of the responsibilities which are to be discharged. Then it confers on the parents an intimate and more efficacious authority in the upbringing of their children, while children and young people, as they grow older, judge appropriately the true goods

Human life is not to be considered as a problem or a disease. Yet, it is not even a 'right' in the strict sense, not even of properly married couples who deeply wish to have children. Such couples have a true right and a duty to engage in those acts (conjugal acts), which can be the source, at the human level, of a new human life, acts which should express and deepen their love for one another and unite them more closely together (their unitive meaning) and which may be the source 'at the human level' of new life which comes from the creative act of God, with whom the spouses collaborate in a privileged way. Human life can never be a true 'right' even of a married couple, but will always remain a 'gift' (a 'gift of life' or *donum vitae*); a true right to a child as such would reduce a human being to the level of an 'object'. The increasing separation of human procreation from its proper place in marriage and as the fruit of the marital act was neither foreseen nor wanted by many who favoured contraception, but contraception has facilitated such developments.

Single parents can bring up children well, with heroic sacrifice and exemplary care, when a spouse has died or been abandoned by the other. Foster parents and orphanages have cared well for children entrusted to them. Children who are born need to be looked after and, if their own parents either cannot or do not look after them properly, it is better for them to be looked after by one of their proper parents or by others (principle of subsidiarity), in line with morally proper regulation by the public authorities in the direct interests of the children themselves. This is an aspect of the good of the child (*'bonum prolis'*) promoted by Catholic doctrine and pastoral practice for centuries. Very different is a massive experiment in social engineering, reflected in and stimulated by cultural changes, frequently negative media presentations of marriage and family, and powerful ideological and political forces opposed to marriage in principle. The first victims of such experimentation are children themselves. Marriage, as the life-long union of one man and one woman, open to children, is the only proper 'place' into which to bring new

of the person and exercise, calmly and in a suitable manner, strength of mind and of the senses.

human life into existence, to nurture and bring up the children born to their parents. Only where the couple cannot or do not fulfil their responsibilities should others operate in their place ('*in loco parentum*').

After underlining the true goods of human life, including its procreation, and marriage, Paul VI identifies chastity as the key to seeing the point of the doctrine of this encyclical and living according to it. It involves the practice of 'self-control' over the passions.

The 'meanings of love proper to the conjugal life' are the unitive and procreative meanings, key goods to be appreciated, to help people to accept and follow the norms (right moral order) taught in the encyclical. Talk of 'self-control' or 'perfect control' of the 'urges of nature' or of the 'passions', exercised through 'reason and free will' (n. 21) can give a misleadingly negative impression of the positive virtue of chastity. Sexual urges, passions or instincts in our bodies do certainly call for self-control (n. 10); this is true in respect of responsible parenthood, but it is true of all of us. Our sexuality is part of God's good creation (Gen. 1:26-28; 2:23-24) and the natural inclination rooted in it directs the human race in general towards the sexual communion of male and female in marriage and to the generation of new life as goods to be pursued and respected, although some individuals, while respecting and promoting these goods, will not actively participate in their concrete realisation (i.e., will not marry and have children) because they are not called to the marital vocation. The urges or passions, then, as such are God-given, are orientated towards the goods and meanings of which we have spoken and are themselves good. However, as with everything else, the impact of the Fall means that our passions or urges do not remain always or easily aligned to the goods towards which they are orientated. For those who are not believers, this truth can be perceived from the experience that in every sphere of life, our inclinations and urges to the moral good are often weakened by contrasting inclinations of passions or urges to do what is wrong, merely convenient and pleasurable instead of what is good and right.

Betrayal in marriage, aggression, exploitation, commercial and other abuse in the sexual sphere are all constant reminders that the Church's Magisterium is being simply realistic in noting these realities.

Chastity is living rightly as sexual beings, respecting ourselves and others by what we say and do as sexual beings. Therefore, it implies never directly and deliberately violating any of the sexual goods, of marriage (by adultery or lust after another's spouse), of procreation (by direct abortion, direct sterilisation or contraception, conceiving children outside of marriage or by replacing the conjugal act), or by any other form of sexual abuse of self or of others. These are negative aspects and entail serious obligations, but they are analogous to the serious negative obligations pertaining to the virtue of justice (never directly, deliberately killing an innocent human being, never deliberately stealing or defrauding another, never committing perjury, etc.). No such negative aspects will ever produce virtue, but they are necessary parts of developing virtue. The deliberate, persevering pursuit of the goods of marriage, of the love of the couple for one another and of their children, of the good of life, of procreation and of the upbringing of children is part of that task.

The benefits of such virtuous living are: peace and tranquillity, assistance in resolving difficulties, caring for and protecting one another as spouses, overcoming undue concern with self, reinforcing authority as parents, enabling children and young people to appreciate and live in a way which respects the dignity of persons. Such benefits are neither automatic nor easily assured, but, contrasted with the pain and harm of adultery, abuse and neglect, are worth striving for through the practice of chastity.

If contraception is to be avoided as incompatible with the virtue of chastity, conversely, chastity is to be practised more generally in order to make the avoidance of this moral wrong more easily realisable. Its practice implies avoiding the conjugal act, for serious reasons (n. 10), at times of the cycle when the wife is judged to be fertile. It implies avoiding excessive or

(Creating an Environment Favourable to Chastity)

22. § 1 In fact, making the most of this opportunity, we wish to admonish educators and all those whose right and duty it is to advance the common good of human society of the need to bring about a state of affairs which favours the development of chastity, in such a way that an authentic freedom may conquer licence, as the norms of the moral order have been clearly observed.

§ 2 Therefore, whatever disturbs the senses through what today are called the instruments of social communication and whatever feeds dissolute morals, be that any obscenity in the written word or any form of degrading performances, are to be rejected openly and with one voice by all those who are bound by the responsibility both for promoting civic culture and for safeguarding

disordered ways of acting sexually, as the sexual inclination or passion has itself been disordered by the Fall. Positively, the married couple exercise chastity, when they – to show their love for one another in other, morally upright ways at fertile times of the cycle – take deliberate care of one another's feelings and of their love for each other, enable this variety in the expression of their love to become something positive, and look forward to other times in the cycle when they will be able again to express their love through the conjugal act itself. Both abstinence in the fertile times and recourse to the conjugal act in infertile times are positive acts of responsible parenthood, fully respecting both the unitive and procreative meanings of their marriage and of their conjugal acts, even though these latter are chosen so that they will not be procreative in fact at that time. Both respect fully the virtue of marital chastity.

22. This paragraph begins a series of appeals by Pope Paul to various groups, here first of all to those involved in education at any level. The appeal is to foster the conditions for the promotion of the virtue of chastity, as part of the common good of society. The role of the virtue of chastity is indispensable in this task.

We only have to think of the sexual abuse of the human person to know that this is a real, important moral concern, for any parents and for any society, not just for the Church. Allowing ourselves to be dominated by any immoral or disordered passion is bad; in our time, we know all too well what great damage can be done to people where this aspect of sexual living is neglected. Freedom is neither licence to do as we please, not even with the consent of another, nor is it possible where we are slaves to sexual urges or passions and demean ourselves and others as a result.

The responsibility of all involved in education is engaged here. There is a particular appeal to avoid damaging morals through written materials, public performances or other forms of mass communication. It is a call to civic responsibility, with a note that artistic licence does not justify incorporating the highest goods of the mind. For a person acts wrongly who strives to approve of depravities of this sort, seeking justification for this on the basis of artistic and scientific worth[25] or on the basis of arguments from liberty of expression which public authorities perhaps may allow in this area.

(*Appeal to Public Authorities*)

23. § 1 So, therefore, we are happy to address the rulers of the nations, on whom to be sure is laid the very heavy burden of safeguarding the common good and, we may be allowed to add, all the more the safeguarding of good morals. (We urge) that they never permit the upright morals of their peoples to be corrupted; especially that, through laws relating to the family which is the primary cell of the State, they prevent the introduction of practices which go against natural and divine law. For civil authority both can and ought to resolve the question about the increase of population in another way; clearly, that of introducing prudent laws regarding families and instructing peoples so wisely that both the moral law and civil liberty are safeguarded.

---

[25] Cf. Second Vatican Council, Decree *Inter mirifica*, nn. 6-7, A.A.S., LVI (1964), p. 147.

material which undermines public morality (n. 22 § 2). The long debate over artistic licence and public morality continues. However, episodes of young people killing many innocent people in colleges after watching videos, and sex offenders feeding their proclivities off television, video and internet productions of a pornographic nature, ought to give real cause to challenge seriously the dominant liberal presumptions of recent decades. The presentation of marriage and of family life in the media in recent years has done much not just to present problems, but to cultivate an attitude of excessive criticism, if not of actual denigration, of these foundational realities of any society. The current tendency, ideologically motivated, to present all forms of sexuality as morally equivalent and worthy is a further step in this direction.

23. This appeal is to public authorities. Governments are urged to fulfil their duty to act in favour of the common good and so to protect marriage and the family, the basic, primary cell of society.

§ 2 Yet, we know well how great a cause of difficulty this is for the governors of the State, especially in those states which are striving for development. In fact, fully aware of the just concerns by which they are afflicted, We have issued the encyclical letter under the title *Populorum progressio*. Now, though, together with our venerable predecessor, John XXIII, we repeat these words: "these questions ... are to be resolved in such a way that people adopt neither ways of acting nor reasons for acting which are contrary to their dignity, approaches which those people have no scruples about advocating, who judge that the person as such and human life are to be referred in all their parts to mere matter. Thus, we judge that this question can only be resolved, if developments in economic and social affairs protect and increase goods worthy of the name, of each individual citizen and of the whole human race."[26] Indeed, this cannot be done without grave injustice if responsibility is attributed to divine providence which, on the contrary, is seen to proceed from the less wise reasoning of those governing the State, or from a certain reductive sense of social justice or from using the goods (of the earth) on the basis of their own convenience, or finally, from irresponsible neglect in undertaking the efforts and burdens needed by which a people and all its children may

---

[26] Encyclical letter, *Mater et Magistra*, A.A.S., LIII (1961), p. 447.

Quoting John XXIII and Paul VI's *Populorum progressio* of 1967, governments are reminded that real worries about large populations and about ensuring adequate development for them should never lead to the imposition of immoral, unjust practices (abortion, sterilisation, contraception are in mind). Other methods of ensuring food and broader economic and integral development can be used (e.g., vast resources wasted on the arms race could be diverted to these purposes, bringing infertile areas into cultivation, etc.). Great social injustice is done when people are subjected to the immoral measures noted, either directly by governments or indirectly when foisted upon people by national or international bodies through development programmes. The Pope also notes the injustice of attributing lack of development to God or to providence, where it is the result of irrational or unjust moral choices (perhaps the option to pursue arms rather than authentic human development).

be led to a higher standard of living.[27] Would that the world's authorities, in whose power this matter lies, as some of them already do so very well, may actively renew their efforts in what they have already begun and in what they have undertaken to do. Nor is the endeavour to provide mutual aid between all parts of the great human family to be deferred. Indeed, we think the area in which the greatest institutions belonging to many nations can make a contribution is almost unlimited.

(*To Scientists*)

24. Now, however, it is pleasing that men who study the sciences should follow the words of our exhortation, 'since they may be able to be of great service to the good of marriage and of the family and the peace of consciences, if, pooling together their studies, they strive to elucidate more closely the different conditions favouring the upright regulation of human procreation.'[28] For it is to be wished in the first place, which earlier was the wish of Pius XII, that medical skill may be able to establish a sufficiently sure basis, which is found in observing the natural cycles, for the morally upright regulating of children.[29] Thus, indeed,

---

[27] Cf. Encyclical letter, *Populorum progressio*, nn. 48-55, *A.A.S.*, LIX (1967), pp. 281-284.

[28] Second Vatican Council, Pastoral Constitution, *Gaudium et spes*, n. 52, *A.A.S.*, LVIII (1966), p. 1074.

[29] Allocution to the Conference of the Association known as 'Family Front' and to the Association of Large Families, *A.A.S.*, XLIII (1951), p. 859.

24. The next appeal, to scientists, is not an afterthought, following a difficult teaching in the encyclical. It follows Pius XII's call to medical scientists to examine these questions to give spouses a more reliable way of identifying the infertile phases of the cycle and that of the Second Vatican Council to scientists to explore upright ways of facilitating responsible parenthood. Paul VI again cites the Council when he states that "there can be no true conflict between the divine laws of transmitting life and those of the fostering of genuine conjugal love" (n. 24).

A commentary on the encyclical cannot be turned into a handbook on what is often called 'natural family planning'. A few general points, however, should be noted:

    – For reasons explained above, this is not a question of 'mere method', nor is it a question of 'natural' versus 'artificial' (see above re nn. 14, 16).

    – The Church's Magisterium has not given directions as to which 'methods' should or may be used, but has taught moral norms. Provided the intention complies with the criteria in n. 10 of the encyclical and provided what is done does not violate any moral norms forbidding that

learned men and women, those especially who are dignified with the name of Catholic, will show by the work they have done, that, as the Church teaches, 'there can be no true contradiction between the divine laws of transmitting life and those of the fostering of genuine conjugal love.'[30]

---

[30] Second Vatican Council, Pastoral Constitution, *Gaudium et spes*, n. 51, *A.A.S.*, LVIII (1966), p. 1072.

which is morally wrong, including all contraception (n. 14), the particular (so-called natural) 'method' may be chosen which best suits the couple.

– In fact, the methods known to date which are compatible with what is morally right are really 'diagnostic techniques'; in and of themselves, they do nothing to seek or avoid a pregnancy, but they give the married couple information about the time of fertility of the wife, whether she is in the fertile or in the infertile phase of her cycle. The properly moral judgment and behaviour then has to be chosen by the couple, as explained earlier.

– The Ogino-Knaus method or 'rhythm method' as such was a recognition that there were fertile and infertile times in the cycle, but how to identify which was which was not so easy or reliable eighty years ago. The basal body temperature method discovered in the middle of the last century involved the wife taking her temperature each morning to try to identify when ovulation (fertility) was occurring, since there would be a notable rise in the temperature of the body at rest, although this could be masked by temperature rises caused by illness. One of the main results of scientific investigation of these matters, undertaken in response to the appeals of the Magisterium, was the discovery of the so-called ovulation or Billings method in 1971, involving an examination of cervical mucus by the wife, where thick, dry mucus indicates infertility and thin, wet mucus fertility (taught successfully to illiterate peoples on that basis). Charting the cycle and coming to know the normal pattern of fertility/ infertility in the individual woman's cycle is part of learning this way of identifying fertility/ infertility more easily. The sympto-thermal method involves detecting and interpreting a combination of factors indicating fertility/ infertility, including cervical mucus and basal body temperature. If we were to prescind from what is morally right and just consider efficiency for a moment, it is worth noting that, properly used, these methods (ovulation and

sympto-thermal), are as successful in identifying fertility/infertility and in enabling a married couple with an upright intention of responsible parenthood to avoid pregnancy as is the contraceptive pill when used 'correctly'.

– None of these methods damage the woman; they are diagnostic methods. Acting upon the information they provide in a way which is morally upright, avoiding abortion, sterilisation and contraception, but using the infertile periods for conjugal intercourse and other ways of expressing conjugal love in the fertile periods of the cycle, no damage is done to the woman's health. The systematic interference with the vagina by the use of an IUD, the systematic chemical deception involved in the use of the pill over time, to deceive the body's mechanisms into thinking ovulation has occurred and into blocking it where the pill acts as a contraceptive or to interfere on a regular basis with the formation of the placenta to render it inhospitable to the newly conceived human being and so to provoke an abortion, are avoided. This means that there are no long-term cancer risks nor problems of infertility consequent upon long-term contraception which then make it very difficult for women to conceive later on when they wish to do so.

– A married couple seeking to have a child, though having no 'right' as such to have a child, can use these diagnostic techniques to identify the best time to seek to have a child.

– Periodic continence or abstinence has often been found to improve communication between married couples on what matters in their lives, as dialogue is needed about their intimate relationship, and to foster more deliberate care of one another. This is not automatic, but it contrasts with taking one another for granted or treating one another routinely or casually, which can happen if contraception becomes a habit. Dialogue and care are real possibilities, worth pursuing deliberately as part of periodic continence.

(*To Christian Spouses*)

25. § 1 Now, in fact, our prayer is directed in a special way to our sons and daughters, to those especially whom God calls to serve him in the state of marriage. For the Church, while she hands on the conditions of divine law inviolate, announces salvation and opens the ways of grace through the sacraments by which a person is made a new creature, who responds in charity and in true liberty to the supreme plan of their Creator and Saviour and who also feels the yoke of Christ to be gentle.[31]

§ 2 Therefore, following his voice modestly, Christian spouses recall that their vocation to the Christian life, which arises from baptism, is further elaborated and confirmed in the sacrament of marriage. They themselves 'are strengthened and as it were consecrated' by the same sacrament, so that they may carry out their responsibilities faithfully, that they may pursue their vocation to its fulfilment and that they may put forward a Christian witness before the world, as is appropriate for them.[32] For the Lord entrusts such a responsibility to them, so that they may reveal to people the holiness and at the same time the

---

[31] Cf. Mt. 11: 30.
[32] Second Vatican Council, Pastoral Constitution, *Gaudium et spes*, n. 48, A.A.S., LVIII (1966), pp. 1067-1069; Dogmatic Constitution, *Lumen gentium*, n. 35, A.A.S., LVII (1965), pp. 40-41.

25. This appeal is directed to Christians, especially to Christian spouses. The Pope, recalling the Church's task of announcing salvation and opening the way to grace through the sacraments, reminds Christian spouses, initiated into the life of Christ through baptism, that they are consecrated "as it were" as spouses through the sacrament of matrimony. People are consecrated to Christ through baptism, a consecration strengthened through confirmation. Specific vocations to the consecrated life involve a consecration by vows or another form of profession of the evangelical counsels of poverty, chastity and obedience, and there is too the specific, priestly consecration of a man through the sacrament of Holy Orders in the priestly and episcopal degrees. The marriage of two baptised persons is judged by the Catholic Church to be a sacrament, that of matrimony.

To say such spouses are further consecrated 'as it were' through the sacrament of matrimony reflects an early call by Pius XI to spouses to grow in sanctity in *Casti connubii* (1930), but especially the Second Vatican Council's teaching that matrimony for two baptised persons is a specific vocation in the Church, something not adequately appreciated previously, where vocations were often presented as though they concerned only the call to the priesthood or to the religious life.[73]

A sacramental marriage, like all sacraments, bestows upon those who receive it, the couple (unless blocked by their personal sin), the grace of God. The Blessed Trinity dwells within them, to strengthen them with that divine presence which is more powerful than human weakness. This also recalls the doctrine that those who have truly received a particular vocation from Christ receive the particular graces which will enable them, despite their own weaknesses, to live

---

[73] Cf. Second Vatican Council, Dogmatic Constitution on the Church, *Lumen gentium*, n. 35; Decree on the Lay Apostolate, *Apostolicam actuositatem*, n. 11.

gentleness of his law, by which their mutual love is united, with their active cooperation, to the love of God, the author of human life.

§ 3 In no way at all do we wish to be silent about the difficulties, at times serious, into which the life of Christian spouses runs; for to them, as to each one of us, 'the gateway is narrow and the road difficult, which leads to life'.[33] Nevertheless, in the hope of this life, their path may be illuminated as though by a very bright light, while they struggle with a strong mind, 'that they may live in this world soberly, justly and in holiness',[34] recognising clearly that 'the form of this world is passing away'.[35]

§ 4 For this reason let spouses willingly accept the labours destined for them, strengthened both by faith and by that hope 'which does not delude because the love of God has been poured into our hearts by the Holy Spirit who has been given to us';[36] then by assiduous prayer, let them implore divine help and especially may they draw grace and love from the perennial fount of the Eucharist. If, however, they are still held down by sins, let them not become despondent in their minds, but let them take refuge constantly and humbly in the mercy of God which the sacrament of penance pours out in

---

[33] Mt. 7: 14; cf. Heb. 12: 11.
[34] Cf. Tit. 2: 12.
[35] Cf. 1 Cor. 7: 31.
[36] Rom. 5: 5.

out that vocation faithfully. We might put it like this: such a couple receive the grace of the sacrament of matrimony not just on their wedding day, but they receive it on their wedding day for the rest of their lives, their union with one another being strengthened by a real, invisible sacramental union with Christ, the Lord, to unite them more deeply to one another and to him, to sustain and nurture them in their times of joy and in the difficulties of their life. The Pope makes specific reference to those responsibilities of their married state, already stated as God's law, that "their married love may be united, with their active cooperation, to the love of God, the author of life" (n. 25 § 1), responsibilities for which this grace is given to them.

None of this is to pretend that the difficulties of the married are not real or that they are always slight, but couples are exhorted to follow with determination the narrow path which leads to life (n. 25 § 2). Very importantly, Paul VI encourages Christian spouses to persevere, with the aid of prayer and of the sacraments, especially those of reconciliation (penance, confession) and Holy Communion (n. 25 § 4). This is so that they may not become despondent in the face of difficulties.

The specific difficulties of spouses who find the teaching of this encyclical hard to understand or to accept or to live out is certainly part of what Pope Paul had in mind. Catholic spouses are in mind when he speaks of these two sacraments (since other Christians are not normally able to be admitted to them). The pastoral encouragement given to spouses here is linked to a clear doctrine, not just of the moral norms taught earlier in the encyclical, although certainly they are included, being part of the "conditions of the divine law inviolate" (n. 25 § 1). Rather, this pastoral appeal is addressed to people, even if "they are still held down by their sins" (n. 25 § 3), who are urged to approach God's mercy in the sacrament of reconciliation, to "take refuge" there "constantly and humbly" in order to be able to come to the perfection of the conjugal life. Here we see a pastoral approach, which recognises human weakness, which is concerned to help spouses to progress, even if they

abundance. Truly in this way they will be able to come to the perfection of the conjugal life, which the Apostle expounds in these words: 'Husbands love your wives just as Christ loved the Church ... In the same way also husbands must love their wives as their own bodies. Whoever loves his wife loves himself. For no-one ever hates his own body, but nourishes it and protects it, just as Christ does the Church... this sacrament is great and indeed I say that it applies to Christ and to the Church. Indeed, you individually, each one of you, let him love his wife as he loves himself; let the wife however respect her husband.'[37]

(*Family Apostolate*)

26. However, of the fruits which mature if the divine law is kept with a sincere intention of the mind, the most outstanding indeed is found, and not rarely, when spouses themselves wish to share their experience with other spouses. Hence, it happens that by the very breadth of the vocation of the laity a certain new and distinctive type of apostolate is included by which like serve like. For the spouses themselves engage in an apostolic service (*munus*) to other spouses, to whom they offer themselves as guides. In truth, this appears today to be most appropriate among so many forms of Christian apostolate.[38]

---

[37] Eph. 5: 25, 28-29, 32-33.
[38] Second Vatican Council, Dogmatic Constitution, *Lumen gentium*, nn. 35

fail and even if they fail repeatedly. Their 'humble' seeking of forgiveness, as with any sin, implies their willingness to try to live better lives, even though it may be foreseen that this may be hard, even if further lapses are possible or even likely, provided that this sincere desire to live better, to leave behind what is morally wrong, is there. This sorrow and firm purpose of amendment are always to be presumed in the penitent. Such spouses are urged to draw strength from the "perennial fount of the Eucharist", so that their conversion and the living out of their marital responsibilities both in regard to the duties pertaining to the unitive meaning of their life and of their acts and as to their procreative meaning may be assisted by the Lord Himself. Far from any harsh rejection, the Pope calls on couples to conversion to what is right, and to avail themselves in this task of the merciful love of God.

26. This brief appeal concerns the apostolate of the married couple, linked to their specific vocation to marriage. The Christian married couple have the task of spreading the Gospel precisely through being a married couple and family. Living out that vocation, living faithful, life-long, loving lives as a couple, open to new life from God and raising any children born with care, is itself a living witness to the Gospel and specifically to the Gospel about marriage, the gift of new human life and the family.

The Pope encourages Christian married couples to share their experiences with one another, since this can be a very important way of helping others to see the value of such a life and vocation. It is precisely this type of apostolate that has helped many couples, either from the start or after difficulties have arisen, even after many years using contraceptives, to take seriously and to embrace ways of living out the duties of responsible parenthood which are morally upright. Couples who use, know and esteem the ovulation method,

(To Doctors and to Medical Personnel)

27. Equally, we show respect to doctors and to those who serve the profession of healing, who, each discharging their particular responsibility, strive to protect those things which the character of their Christian vocation especially demands from them, rather than serving some form of human interest. Therefore, may they persevere constantly in their commitment of always promoting those schemes which adhere both to faith and to right reason and may they strive for that purpose that they may obtain agreement and observance of those same values from within their own specific community (from among their own colleagues). Moreover, may they hold it as a special responsibility of their profession to obtain for themselves the necessary knowledge of the science of this most difficult area, so that they may be able truly to give correct advice to spouses seeking their opinion and to show them the right way, which in law and in fact are expected of them.

---

and 41, *A.A.S.*, LVII (1965), pp. 40-45; Pastoral Constitution, *Gaudium et spes*, nn. 48-49, *A.A.S.*, LVIII (1966), pp. 1067-70; Decree, *Apostolicam actuositatem*, n. 11, *A.A.S.*, LVIII (1966), pp. 847-849.

the sympto-thermal method, etc., help others to understand it, not as a mere method, but within the context of the goods and meaning of marriage, within a positive appreciation of the virtue of chastity, as a way of leading a happy and successful married life together.

27. This appeal is to doctors and to other medical personnel. In the first place, they are urged always to fulfil their professional duties, with full respect for what is required by their vocation as Christians, using practices which "adhere both to faith and to right reason" (n. 27). The Pope exhorts them to do this, especially those more directly involved in those areas of the profession which relate to the issues discussed in the encyclical, so that they may give proper advice to married couples who consult them, indicating to them the right way to act. They are particularly encouraged to investigate further the scientific aspects "of this most difficult area", in a way that gains them respect from their colleagues (in other words, in a way which is scientifically valid and reliable). Such improvement in knowledge would help them also to give correct advice to patients, as noted.

This paragraph is similar to the appeal made to scientists (n. 24). As mentioned above, much progress has been made in these areas, concerning what is often called 'natural family planning'. The prejudice against such investigations and against using the knowledge gained on the part of couples and doctors is enormous. The 'contraceptive mentality' has made great strides in recent decades and is often taken for granted as correct by many. Nevertheless, the results of the scientific research encouraged by the various Popes has had to be acknowledged, albeit grudgingly. It finds its way into introductory textbooks in biology and even in religious studies, often under a list of methods of contraception, showing that the authors have failed completely to understand that it is nothing of the sort. In a world where 'green issues' are proclaimed as the way forward, the findings of such researchers and practitioners, of true value for people in all cultures, can help to foster what John Paul II called an

(*To Priests*)

28. Full of great confidence, we appeal to you, beloved sons who are priests, who, by the sacred responsibility which you fulfil, act as advisers and as spiritual leaders both of individuals and of families. For it is your primary duty – we speak especially to you who teach moral theology – to put forward in its entirety and openly the doctrine of the Church on marriage. You (are to be) the first, in discharging your ministry, to provide an example of the sincere obedience (*obsequium*) which is to be given, interiorly and exteriorly, to the ecclesiastical Magisterium. For you know that you are bound by such obedience not so much on the basis of those arguments which are put forward (for a particular teaching), but on account of the light of the Holy Spirit, which the pastors of the Church enjoy in a special way when explaining the truth.[39] Nor does it escape you all that it is of the greatest importance, for the sake of the peace of souls and of the unity of the Christian people, in moral matters as in matters of dogma, that all submit to the

---

[39] Cf. Second Vatican Council, Dogmatic Constitution, *Lumen gentium*, n. 25, *A.A.S.*, LVII (1965), pp. 29-31.

"authentic human ecology", whose "first point of reference is the family".[74]

28. The Pope turns now to priests, in paragraphs 28 and 29. Priests as spiritual guides and as teachers, especially priests involved in teaching moral theology, are urged as their "primary duty":

– "to put forward in its entirety and openly the doctrine of the Church on marriage"

– to provide a sincere example of obedience, interior and exterior, to the Magisterium

– to be united in giving this message to people, to foster peace and unity among Christian people, on matters of faith, but also on matters of moral doctrine (n. 28).

Many priests at the time were caught in the general reaction of people who thought there might have been a change in the Church's doctrine and who were not prepared for the encyclical when it emerged. Leaving aside those who may have reacted in a contentious manner, it would be true to say that many priests trained for the priesthood much earlier might not have known the precise detail of the matter confronted in the encyclical, while those who had been in seminaries during the years of the Council might have been encouraged to think in terms of a change of doctrine. After the Council, seminaries were in a state of uncertainty, since there was so much from the Council that was new or set within a new framework that what had been done before seemed inadequate, but no reliable new course books and programmes had yet been devised. The pastoral crisis resulting from reactions to this encyclical arose within this context of confusion. In the resulting turmoil, perhaps many did not read Pope Paul's text, but only inadequate renditions of it or, worse, attacks upon it in the press.

Paul VI's call to priests to obedience and to unity in presenting this doctrine in its entirety was thoroughly

---

[74] John Paul II, Encyclical letter, *Centesimus annus*, nn. 38-39.

Magisterium of the Church and be united in what they say. For this reason, making use of the demanding words of the great Apostle Paul, we appeal to you again with our whole heart: 'I beseech you ..., brothers, through the name of our Lord, Jesus Christ, that you all teach the same doctrine and there be no schisms among you, that you may be united in the same opinion and in the same judgment.'[40]

---

[40] I Cor. 1: 10.

legitimate. One way to ensure that, might have been for bishops to have organised gatherings for priests led by moral theologians who understood and who accepted the doctrine taught. The trouble was that some of the moral theologians, some of whom had been part of the majority group on the Papal Commission before the encyclical, had either become so convinced of their view of things that they could not in conscience reconsider them or openly challenged the doctrine of the encyclical. This left bishops and priests in a predicament.

It cannot be said that the years which followed improved matters. A number of moralists who could not or would not accept the Church's moral doctrine focused on other areas of moral theology. Soon much attention was being given to what is called 'fundamental moral theology', to the underlying principles of all moral theology. Here some of the ideas which had surfaced in the Papal Commission and which had been explicitly rejected by Paul VI in this encyclical (cf. n. 14) were elaborated and put forward with ever greater conviction as a new way of doing morality. Priests were often trained in these new approaches in the decades which followed. Despite increasingly numerous and solid arguments from other moral theologians, criticising the newer, relativistic approach which these moralists had fostered, their willingness to listen was very restricted indeed. Eventually, John Paul II issued a major encyclical on the principles of moral theology, *Veritatis splendor* (1993), to state clearly what was and what was not compatible with Catholic moral doctrine.

Regrettably, the confusion after *Humanae vitae* led many priests to be silent about the teachings of the encyclical. Out of pastoral concern, others gave people advice incompatible with the truth it proclaims, but to hear what you wish to hear is not always to hear what is right or helpful. Paul VI speaks of the duty of priests to given obedient assent to the teachings of the encyclical (n. 28). The status of the teaching or doctrine needs to be examined in its own right and comments will be made in the general reflection on the encyclical, later in this

29. § 1 Further, if it is the distinguishing nature of the love of souls to omit nothing from the saving doctrine of Christ, yet it is necessary that the same doctrine always be joined with tolerance and with charity, of which the Redeemer himself offered examples in what he said and in what he did among people. For since he came not to condemn the world, but to save it,[41] he was indeed harshly severe towards sins, but patient and merciful towards sinners.

§ 2 Therefore, burdened by their difficulties, may spouses find expressed in the words and in the heart of the priest, as it were, the image of the voice and of the love of our Redeemer.

§ 3 For may you speak full of confidence, beloved sons, certainly holding that the Holy Spirit of God, while present to the Magisterium as it proclaims right doctrine, illuminates the hearts of the faithful from within and invites them to give their assent to it. Indeed, teach spouses the necessary way of praying and establish them properly so that they may approach more often the sacraments of the Eucharist and of Penance with faith, so that they may never lose heart through their weakness.

---

[41] Cf. Jn. 3: 17.

book, as to what response is due to that teaching, not just from priests, but from all.

29. The Pope continued to link clear doctrine with compassionate, pastoral concern. As he said himself, he could do no better than emulate Christ, firm in doctrine, but tolerant and compassionate (n. 29). Paul VI reminded priests that the Holy Spirit who assisted the Church in its proclamation of doctrinal truth, also worked in the hearts of people to help them to assent to it (which does not mean that it becomes untrue if they do not assent to it!) In harmony with what he had said to Christian spouses (n. 25), he encouraged priests to guide people with compassion and to encourage them to make use of the sacrament of penance and of the Eucharist.

(*To Bishops*)

30. But now, concluding this encyclical letter, we turn our mind respectfully and lovingly to you, beloved and venerable brothers who have the responsibility of being bishops, you with whom we share more closely the cares of the spiritual good of the People of God. For we invite you all by this urgent appeal, that, leading your priests, your collaborators in the sacred ministry and your faithful, you may attend with all energy and without delay to the safeguarding of marriage and to proclaiming its holiness, by which the conjugal life may attain all the more to its human and Christian perfection. Hold this indeed as the greatest work and task entrusted to you in this present time. For, as you know well, the same responsibility demands a certain ordering (priority) of the pastoral ministry as that which applies to all areas of human activity, such as to economic affairs, good teaching and social questions. If these all make more progress and if they progress at the same time, they not only render the life of parents and of children in the intimate fold of the family more tolerable, but easier and at the same time happier. Thus, living together in human society is made more fruitful by fraternal charity and safer by a true peace, when the plan which God conceived in his mind for the world is observed in holiness.

30. This appeal is addressed to the Pope's 'brothers in the episcopate', the bishops. They are urged, together with their priests, to strive energetically to see to it that the doctrine on marriage and on the conjugal life was made known. He asked them to give this matter priority in their pastoral care, so that people could live in their families in peace and happiness.

(*Final Appeal*)

31. We now call You, venerable brothers, you beloved sons (priests), all you people of good will, to the truly great work of education, of development and of charity, relying on the very firm doctrine of the Church, which the Successor of Peter, one with his brothers in the Catholic episcopate, faithfully guards and interprets. That really great work, as we ourselves are firmly persuaded, turns out for the good both of the world and of the Church, since people cannot come to true happiness, which they should seek with all the powers of their soul, unless they observe the laws inscribed by the supreme God in their own human nature, which are to be implemented prudently and lovingly. Therefore, for such a great task we implore from God, most holy and most merciful, the abundance of heavenly graces both for you all and especially for spouses as a sign of which we willingly impart to you our Apostolic Blessing.

Given at Rome, at St Peter's, on the 25th day of the month of July, on the feast of St James the Apostle, in the year 1968, the sixth of our Pontificate,

Pope Paul VI.

HUMANAE VITAE: COMMENTARY

31. The final appeal is to all in the Church and, as at the beginning, to all "of good will". Reminding us that he was speaking as "the Successor of Peter", as Pope, but in union with the bishops of the Catholic Church, Pope Paul repeats the function of the Magisterium (Pope and bishops in communion with him) to "guard and interpret" Church doctrine. This is done for the good not only of the Church, but of the world, of all people, since it is impossible to reach true happiness if the laws of God are not observed. The reference to all people of good will and to God's laws also being those written in our nature (natural moral law) recurs. However, the encyclical is at the service of promoting people's true happiness (not to be reduced to what they want or desire). That happiness directly concerns spouses and what is needed for a good and happy married life. Proclaiming God's law, what is right and wrong, is to teach what truly facilitates a happiness not limited to this world, but which is to be fulfilled in the next. The moral life is not mainly a question of following laws or rules, but living by these in order to do what is good and right and to share in the blessed happiness and goodness of God's own life.

The encyclical concludes with the Pope imparting his Apostolic Blessing.

APPENDIX

GENERAL COMMENTARY

1. Introduction

The pastoral crisis which emerged after the publication of *Humanae vitae* is well known. There were attempts to assess the status of the teaching it contained and thus the extent to which it was binding in conscience. Efforts by bishops to respond to the confusion among people who had expected a change of doctrine, or at least that the new anovulant pill might be accepted as morally licit, were affected by confusion among some of them too. Some urged that people 'follow their conscience', which expresses a moral duty upon all of us, but which in itself is ambiguous. Some theologians, convinced that a different teaching ought to have been given, pursued a number of the ideas which had emerged in the majority group on the Papal Commission prior to the encyclical, which led to an extension of the tension and crisis to the whole area of fundamental moral theology in the years which followed. Other theologians sought to understand and explain the doctrine of the encyclical and what lay behind it.

Some of these points have emerged in part in the commentary on each paragraph of the encyclical. Here it is intended to look at some questions in a more systematic analysis. The status of the Magisterial teaching in the encyclical, the duties of conscience in regard to that teaching and the foundations of the teaching itself will be examined. There will also be a brief reflection on three issues which have emerged since, upon which the doctrines of the encyclical may have a bearing: assistance to those married couples who seek a child but who have problems of sterility, and the matter of the use of a contraceptive as a defence against sexual aggression and against the aggression of sexually transmitted disease. These questions will be examined in turn.

2. The Status of the Teaching in *Humanae vitae*

The status of the doctrine presented by Paul VI has been debated ever since. If it had been taught infallibly, it would mean that the Pope could not have erred, could not have been wrong, in teaching it because the assistance of the Holy Spirit, promised to the Church and to the Apostles by Jesus, would not have allowed him to teach as true something which in fact was not true. The Holy Spirit maintains the Church in union with Christ throughout the ages, will not allow its faith to fail and will not allow it to teach that something is part of God's revelation if it is not so. Examples of teaching, on matters of faith or morals, given infallibly by the bishops of the Church, in union with the Pope, at a general or ecumenical Council are the dogmas about the Trinity, about Jesus being true God and true man, a divine Person, but with both a divine and a human nature, about the Mass being a true sacrifice, about the Real Presence, about the infallibility of the Pope, etc. Examples of Papal infallibility are the dogmas of the Immaculate Conception and of the Assumption. Most teaching given by the bishops and by the Pope does not come with the guarantee that they could not have been wrong in teaching it, but where they teach on faith or morals as successors of the Apostles (or of St Peter), they are still assisted by the Holy Spirit, even without that guarantee.

In the early years after 1968 it was assumed by most people that the teaching had been put forward in a non-infallible exercise of Papal Magisterium, that the Pope had not defined the doctrine forbidding contraception as a dogma and that the proper moral response to the teaching was that of the '*obsequium religiosum*' (obedience, submission, respect) due to teaching which is proposed without the guarantee of infallibility. Early on there was the claim that Paul VI had taught the doctrine infallibly, since he was giving a definitive judgment on the matter of birth regulation. Then came an attempt to examine the conditions summarised in the Second Vatican Council for teaching which is given infallibly by bishops throughout the world in union with the successor of Peter (the infallibility of the ordinary, universal Magisterium) and to see whether these were verified in the case of the doctrine in the encyclical; a group of theologians and philosophers has become ever more convinced that such conditions are met in this case. There remain very many who do not consider infallibility to be involved and who state that we have to do with non-infallible, but authentic or authoritative Magisterium here. The pastoral significance of these debates is that they affect the response due in conscience to the teaching.

a. Infallibility by Definition of a Dogma
Although it is not necessary for the Magisterium (Bishops in union with the Pope or the Pope as such) to use a particular formula to define a dogma of faith or morals, it has to be clear that this is what they are doing from what is decided in a Council or from what is proclaimed by the Pope. The fact that Paul VI did not use any terminology

in *Humanae vitae* to indicate that he was acting infallibly in proclaiming that doctrine is a strong argument that the doctrine was not so defined. The specific defence of the Magisterium's right and duty to teach in matters of natural moral law (n. 4) could reinforce this impression, since infallibility is limited to what is part of revelation or to what is necessary for the defence or faithful exposition of revelation. For a truth to be defined as a dogma of faith, it has to be part of revelation or necessary to it and is to be believed or held by all the faithful. This was not the case with *Humanae vitae*.

b. Infallibility and Teaching which is Definitive

The view of many people, including many theologians, that *Humanae vitae* is authentic or authoritative, but non-infallibly proposed teaching has led many of them to think that it is not binding in conscience. The view, however, has been put forward that its doctrine is so closely connected to revelation as to be necessary for the defence of what is revealed and was the object of definition by Paul VI.[1] It is not claimed that the teaching is part of revelation itself nor, therefore, that it is a truth defined as dogma to be believed ('*credenda*'), but that it is rooted in natural moral law, which is a reality found in Scripture, and is a doctrine infallibly taught, to be 'held' ('*tenenda*') by all the faithful.

Paul VI intended to settle the question of responsible parenthood which was before him, namely whether the traditional condemnation of contraception covered also the new anovulant pill or whether there might be any exceptions to the rejection of contraception as a morally licit way of regulating births. He referred in the text to the doctrine of the Magisterium being constant (n. 6); in

---

[1] Cf. E. Lio, *Humanae vitae e infallibilità: il Concilio, Paolo VI e Giovanni Paolo II* (Libreria editrice Vaticana, Vatican, 1986).

particular he had referred to the Church not being the author of such doctrine, but only its interpreter, saying she was "unable" to declare morally licit what was of its nature "unchangeably opposed" to the moral good (n. 18). In teaching specifically that all contraception was morally wrong (n. 14), Paul VI was giving a teaching on a matter of morals which was unchangeable or which was definitive, such being clear also from his being "unable" to teach the opposite.

c. Infallibility on the basis of the Ordinary, Universal Magisterium

This point of view was elaborated by J.C. Ford and G. Grisez in an article of 1978 which sought to explore whether or not the conditions for teaching infallibly on this basis had been met in *Humanae vitae*.[2] Here there is neither a question of dogmatic definition, nor of a doctrine being taught definitively and infallibly in the encyclical as such, but rather that the doctrine taught in *Humanae vitae* was already infallibly taught by the bishops throughout the world in their ordinary teaching in union with the Popes; the encyclical then confirmed this teaching.

This suggestion rests on the Second Vatican Council's teaching on the Magisterium. The Magisterium teaches infallibly when proposing a doctrine on faith or morals through a dogmatic definition, or when it teaches such a doctrine in a definitive way when that doctrine is needed to defend or expound revelation, or when the bishops throughout the world, even when not gathered together, concur in a specific judgment about such a doctrine that is to be held ('*tenenda*') definitively and absolutely by the universal Church.[3] For the exercise of infallibility here, it

---

[2] J.C. Ford and G. Grisez, "Contraception and the Infallibility of the Ordinary Magisterium", *Theological Studies*, 39 (1978), 258-312.

[3] Cf. Second Vatican Council, Dogmatic Constitution on the Church, *Lumen*

is not necessary that a doctrine be part of revelation, but that it be necessary for the effective defence or explanation of revelation. It is not necessary that the bishops of the Catholic Church in communion with the Pope meet together, but that they agree (in a moral unanimity) in the same judgment about the matter.[4] It is not even the case that they have to agree now about the doctrine at present, but that there has been agreement about such a doctrine over time in the past; that this was so in respect of the doctrine on contraception across the centuries cannot be doubted.[5] In other words, the dissent of any bishops now would not alter the status of such doctrine as infallibly taught, but would put those bishops entirely at odds with Catholic doctrine. Dissent from others does not affect the question of infallibility in teaching this doctrine by the ordinary, universal Magisterium, since they are not part of the Magisterium.

d. Authentic or Authoritative Teaching, not Infallibly Proposed

This was the interpretation of most people before Ford and Grisez's article and before Lio's book had suggested different reasons for the doctrine to be considered as infallibly taught. This type of Magisterial teaching was also considered at Vatican II and it is the normal way in which the bishops and the Pope exercise their duties of teaching on matters of faith and morals, to keep the Church true to Christ and in communion of faith and life.

The tendency, whether among theologians and others, to judge Paul VI not to have taught infallibly that

---

gentium, n. 25.

[4] Cf. G. Grisez, *The Way of the Lord Jesus*, I, *Christian Moral Principles* (Franciscan Herald Press, Chicago, 1983), 35-D, 843.

[5] Cf. J.T. Noonan, *Contraception, A History of its Treatment by the Catholic Theologians, and Canonists*, enlarged edition (Harvard University Press, Cambridge, Mass., 1986), 6, 539-540.

contraception was always morally wrong and to jump to the conclusion that he might have been in error or even probably had been in error about the doctrine is entirely misguided. It is a logical fallacy to move from there being 'no guarantee of not being wrong' and 'might in theory have been wrong' to 'was likely to have been wrong' or 'was wrong'.[6] The authoritative teaching of the Magisterium carries with it not a presumption of error or of falsehood, but of truth, since the Magisterium is still assisted in such teaching by the Holy Spirit, although without the specific form of that assistance which is entailed in infallibility. For all in the Church and more broadly it constitutes a norm of faith or of morals for their lives.

The Council gave important indications as to how authoritatively proposed doctrine is to be understood and embraced. It will have a higher degree of Magisterial authority depending on what type of document is involved, the frequency with which the doctrine is taught and the terms in which it is taught.[7] Applying these criteria to *Humanae vitae*, it cannot be denied that the document concerned is a Papal encyclical, a teaching document issued to settle this very question relating to contraception, that it confirms constant doctrine repeated across the centuries and that the doctrine is expressed in terms of such action being intrinsically morally wrong, never permissible, not even for very good motives. In other words, the Conciliar criteria imply that, even if the doctrine has not been proposed infallibly,

---

[6] Cf. G.E.M. Anscombe, *Contraception and Chastity* (C.T.S., London, undated), 15. "The fact that" this doctrine may not have been infallibly proposed "shows only that one argument for the truth of its teaching is lacking. It does not show that the substantive hard message of this encyclical may perhaps be wrong – any more than the fact that the memory of telephone numbers is not the *sort* of thing that you *can't* be wrong about shows that you don't actually know your own telephone number." (emphases in the original)

[7] Cf. *Lumen gentium*, n. 25.

it has certainly been proclaimed at the highest level of Magisterial authority and so requires the highest degree of *obsequium*.

e. Infallibly or Authoritatively Proposed Teaching?

Of relevance to this question are at least two later Magisterial interventions, which we shall now examine:

i. John Paul II's Allocution to Moral Theologians, 1988

In connection with a congress to celebrate the twentieth anniversary of *Humanae vitae* and so in direct relationship to the encyclical, Pope John Paul II, spoke to the participants of the responsibility due to Magisterial teaching. He used two key criteria from Vatican II's decree on religious liberty, *Dignitatis humanae*, and added a third. For our purposes here, the important point is that these criteria concern responses to Magisterial teaching which is not infallibly given. Their implications for conscience will be examined below.

ii. The motu proprio *Ad tuendam fidem*, 1998

In 1998 Pope John Paul II issued a legal document, called a *motu proprio* ('by his own movement' or 'hand'), on protecting or safeguarding the faith. *Ad tuendam fidem* changed the 1983 *Code of Canon Law* to incorporate into the law the category of definitive teaching of the Magisterium, in the light of the 1989 Profession of Faith and Oath of Fidelity, required of all being ordained and assuming certain offices in the Church, and making it a canonical crime to deny such truths as definitively taught.[8] Accompanying the promulgation of this text was an 'Explanatory Note' issued by the Congregation for the Doctrine of the Faith, which,

---

[8] John Paul II, Apostolic letter *motu proprio, Ad tuendam fidem*, 28 May, 1988, n. 4 A (c. 750) and B (c. 1371).

amongst other things, gave examples, not complete or exhaustive, of different types or levels of Magisterial teaching. It confirmed the infallibility of the ordinary, universal Magisterium.[9] The question of the doctrine of *Humanae vitae* on contraception is not directly addressed here (nor is it to be expected that it should have been). Clearly, the arguments of Ford and Grisez and others, even that of Lio, are entirely compatible with what is stated there. John Paul II had taught only very recently that the deliberate, direct killing of the innocent human being, directly procured abortion and direct euthanasia were gravely and intrinsically morally wrong, invoking the ordinary universal Magisterium on these matters, in terms reminiscent of the Council's reference to the infallibility of such Magisterium.[10] In the case of euthanasia, there is no direct reference to Scripture; this is an intrinsic moral wrong, whose condemnation is logically connected to the direct killing of the innocent, a doctrine which is rooted in Scripture. The parallel with contraception is clear.

We have seen the assertions of Paul VI that the doctrine on contraception was the constant doctrine of the Church. This is a point of importance both in regard to the claim of infallibility (whether by Lio or by Ford and Grisez and their followers) and in regard to authoritative teaching. Until the Anglican Lambeth Conference of 1930 no Christian Church or ecclesial community had ever taught anything other than its intrinsic moral wrong; not that the Anglican Communion's position affects Catholic doctrine. Corroboration of the constancy of the doctrine came

---

[9] Congregation for the Doctrine of the Faith, Explanatory Note to *Ad tuendam fidem*, nn. 6 and 9.

[10] Cf. John Paul II, Encyclical letter, *Evangelium vitae*, 6 August, 1995, nn. 57, 62 and 65.

from the Greek Orthodox Patriarch, whose remarks, noted earlier, deserve to be presented in a fuller form here:

"I am in agreement with the Pope. *Paul VI could not have expressed any other doctrine* (literally: 'could not have expressed himself differently'). He holds the Gospel in his hands and wishes to save the moral law, the existence of the family and of peoples. I am on the Pope's side in all his acts, his words and his policy."[11]

f. Some further reflections

There have been many attacks by theologians on the doctrine of *Humanae vitae*. It has been argued that most Catholics have simply ignored the teaching, practise contraception, do not mention it in confession and so it cannot be right.[12] The logic of such a position is that the way most people behave must dictate what is morally right and wrong, which would lead to relativism, implying, e.g., that premarital sex was immoral until quite recently, when it became permissible, if not obligatory, simply on the basis of what most people do. It should be noted that, although the infallibility of the Church operates in believing (not in teaching) when everyone from the Pope

---

[11] Statement of Athenagoras, Patriarch of the Greek Orthodox Church, after the encyclical, *Humanae vitae*, 1968. This text appeared in *Herder Korrispondenz*, 22 (1968) and I reproduce it here from an Italian translation of that text, which appears in A. Günthör, "La dottrina della 'Humanae vitae' e il parere di rappresentanti di altre comunità cristiane" in AA.VV. (a cura di), *Humanae vitae: 20 anni dopo: Atti del II Congresso internazionale di teologia morale, Roma 9-12 novembre, 1988* (Ares, Milano, 1989), 515-527 at 517: "Sono d'accordo con il Papa. Paolo VI non poteva esprimersi diversamente. Egli tiene il Vangelo nelle sue mani e vuole salvare la legge morale, l'esistenza della famiglia e dei popoli. Sto dalla parte del Papa in tutti i suoi atti, le sue parole e il suo programma." The emphasis in the English text is mine.

[12] Cf. A. Greeley et al., *Catholic Schools in a Declining Church* (Sheed and Ward, Kansas City, Mo., 1976), 131ff.

to the last member of the faithful concurs in a doctrine to be believed and although the assent of the members of the Church can be a sign of something having been infallibly taught by the Magisterium, the former is not necessary for the latter. Moreover, the common opinion of all the faithful is exercised in harmony with, and never against, Magisterial doctrine, whether infallibly proposed or otherwise.[13]

It has been claimed both that Paul VI was convinced by 1968 that the doctrine on contraception had been taught infallibly by the Magisterium and that the doctrine concerns the lives of so many people at such a basic level that, if this doctrine is not infallibly proposed, then no moral doctrine can be taught infallibly; this on the basis precisely that no moral doctrine can be so taught.[14] At issue is a claim to distinguish absolutely the Holy Spirit and the Church and to insist that any propositions which are needed to express faith and moral truths are necessarily bound to contain falsehood, to be limited by historical perspectives and to be inadequate. Hence, while the Spirit may guarantee that the Church will never fail (indefectibility), teaching infallibly is not possible.[15] This would mean that the Church could not know at any given time what its faith was or whether it was leading people to do moral wrong or right; it also would imply relativism. Apart from the fact that proponents of such views are inclined to exempt their own assertions from such limitations, they fail to distinguish adequately between a truth and its expression; the fact that the latter may be improved or seen within a broader perspective, does not

---

[13] Cf. R. Shaw, "Contraception, Infallibility and the Ordinary Magisterium" in J.E. Smith (ed.), *Why Humanae Vitae was Right: A Reader*, 345-362 at 351-352.
[14] Cf. H. Küng, *Infallible?: An Enquiry* (Doubleday, New York, 1971, 31ff.
[15] Ibid., 181-193.

mean that the truth it contains is false or unknowable. While it is true that the Holy Spirit is not to be identified directly with the Church, Jesus's promise that he would be with the Church until the end of time, means exactly that, guiding the Church and assuring its faith and moral teaching, etc. It is true that the Holy Spirit will ensure the Church does not fail, but, beyond indefectibility, his guidance includes specific assistance to the Magisterium in teaching on faith and morals.

Although there was confusion after the encyclical was issued, the reactions of the Bishops' Conferences were varied. Seeking to help their people in the midst of a pastoral crisis, as Paul VI had urged them to do, bishops in some third world countries welcomed the condemnation of government interference and the insistence of the Pope, as well as of the Council, that couples be responsible for judging the demands of responsible parenthood, according to the norms given. In Spain, where there was little trouble, the emphasis was on the authoritative nature of the encyclical. In Canada and West Germany, the focus was on giving pastoral guidelines, without denying the encyclical's doctrine.[16]

The difficulty was often that bishops did not always grasp the detail of the doctrine or the issues surrounding it, a problem compounded by the dissent of some theologians who might have been advising them. A number of bishops seem to have taken the line of broad

---

[16] Cf. E. Hamel, "Conferentiae episcopales et encyclica *Humanae vitae*", *Periodica de re morali, canonica et liurgica*, 58 (1968), 243-349 at 260-265 (West Germany), 277-281 (Canada), 283-284 (India), 314-318 (Spain); D. Tettamanzi, *La risposta dei vescovi all'Humanae vitae* (Ancora, Milano, 1969), 78-91(West Germany), 136-148 (Canada), 212-222 (Spain); G.J. Woodall, *The Principle of the Indissoluble Link between the Dimensions of Unity and Fruitfulness in Conjugal Love: A Hermeneutical Investigation of its Theological Basis and of its Normative Significance*, excerpt from unpublished doctoral dissertation, (PUG, Roma, 1996), 75-81.

silence, other than trying to maintain unity in the Church by avoiding open dissent and seeking to help people pastorally by urging them to follow their consciences. It is to this aspect we must now turn.

3. The Response due in Conscience to the Teaching

In the turmoil after the encyclical was issued, bishops who advised their people to 'follow your conscience' were stating something true and important, but wholly inadequate. Whether for motives of confusion, fear of aggravating an already difficult pastoral situation or of studied ambiguity, the impression was too easily given that people should 'make up their own minds' about what was the right thing to do in their marriages about responsible parenthood, even that choosing contraception might in some way be morally legitimate if chosen 'in good conscience', although contrary to Magisterial doctrine.

a. Some Remarks on Conscience in General
i. The Second Vatican Council

To understand the role of conscience in this delicate matter, we need to take a step back. The Council had performed a great service in recuperating the religious dimension of conscience more fully when it stated that:

> "Deep within our conscience we find a law which we do not lay upon ourselves, but which we have to obey. Its voice, calling us always to love and to do the good and to avoid what is wrong, where necessary resounds in the ears of our hearts: 'do this', 'avoid that'. For we have a law inscribed in our hearts by God; the very dignity of conscience is to obey that law and, according to that law, we

ourselves shall be judged. Conscience is the most secret centre and sanctuary of the person, in which we find ourselves alone with God, whose voice echoes deep within us. In a wonderful way, in conscience, that law is discovered which is fulfilled in the love of God and of neighbour. Therefore, in fidelity to conscience Christians are joined to other people searching for the truth and in seeking to resolve on the basis of truth the moral problems which arise in the lives of individuals and in groups in society. The more, therefore, a correct conscience prevails, the more individuals and groups draw back from blind choice and strive to conform their behaviour to the objective norms of morality. However, not infrequently, it happens that conscience errs through invincible ignorance, without thereby losing its dignity. That, however, cannot be said when human beings do not take the trouble to enquire about the true and the good and conscience slowly but surely becomes blinded by the habit of sin."[17]

A number of things become clear from reading this passage carefully. On the one hand conscience is a secret sanctuary, in which each person encounters God and his will. Even those who do not believe in God in some way encounter him in conscience; he is the fulness of truth and goodness which they seek when they pursue these sincerely. Each individual seeks truth and moral truth in conscience in a way and at a level which is beyond the direct reach of others, 'on their own' with God. Following conscience requires this personal dialogue with God or reflection on truth; it is

---

[17] Second Vatican Council, Pastoral Constitution on the Church in the Modern World, *Gaudium et spes*, n. 16: my translation, with the use of inclusive language.

the very opposite of seeking what is merely convenient, popular or the result of the habit of sin.

Secondly, conscience necessarily involves openness to truth as an objective reality, to love and do what really is good and to avoid what is morally wrong. This standard or norm of right and wrong is reflected in the law of God or in God's will which conscience does not invent, which human beings do not lay upon themselves, but which is recognised in conscience when this is 'correct' or 'right'.[18] Even for those who do not believe in God, moral goodness and truth, not established by human beings in their fundamental elements, are recognised and pursued, when seeking sincerely and judging correctly in conscience.

It is true that we can be wrong, that conscience can mis-judge situations (conscience is *not* infallible).[19] This can be without any fault on our part, when we could not have known better or when our ignorance is invincible or unconquerable. Respect for our judgment of conscience should remain in such cases, but we are still misguided objectively as to what is truly right or good. This is the basis on which religious liberty is recognised, calling for respect for people who may be in error through no fault of their own, but who have the right to seek the truth about God, to embrace that truth as they see it and to live by it.[20] Where we do not take the trouble to form our conscience correctly, for whatever reason, we act from vincible or conquerable ignorance, which we could and should have avoided and for which we are culpable.

---

[18] Cf. John Paul II, Encyclical letter, *Veritatis splendor*, 6 August, 1993, n. 61.
[19] Cf. ibid., n. 62.
[20] Second Vatican Council, Decree on Religious Liberty, *Dignitatis humanae*, nn. 1, 2 and 10.

ii. Some Misleading Interpretations of the Council's Doctrine

It is seriously mistaken to consider conscience in an individualistic way, as if each person were utterly alone in the face of moral judgments and decisions "in an insurmountable and impenetrable solitude",[21] or as if each person had to invent their own morality.[22] Finding ourselves alone with God in the sanctuary of conscience does mean an intimate relationship with Him which, as such, no-one else can share in the same way, but it does not mean a total isolation. As St Paul indicates (Rom. 2: 12-16), conscience acts as a witness, an interior witness to the truth of what we are doing, seeking the moral good to be done and to identify the moral wrong to be avoided, not seeking or accepting compromises, rationalisations and distortions. The interior dialogue we have with ourselves in conscience is about such goods and truth; it always implies seeking the truth, judging on the basis of truth and acting in accordance with it.[23] As such it opens us up to the fulness of that truth and goodness in God, also in prayer. It unites us with all people of goodwill; here we need to judge in a discriminating way, identifying and resisting individual, group or social pressures to do wrong, accepting genuine criticism so as to re-direct ourselves to what is truly good. All of this is part of the witness of conscience, of its witness to truth and to goodness. In these ways, quite the opposite of the licence to do as we please, as many suggest, 'follow your conscience' is a norm of fundamental significance, to be embraced and pursued. The Magisterium does not replace conscience, but instructs us in conscience,

---

[21] John Paul II, *Veritatis splendor*, n. 58.
[22] Ibid., nn. 60-61.
[23] Cf. ibid., nn. 58, 62.

places before us the truth about the good to be done and the wrong to be avoided, which it does not invent or establish, but which it interprets and teaches; it is an invaluable assistance and service to Christians and to others in the formation of their consciences.[24] It is to be heeded.

b. Conscience and the Norms of Responsible Parenthood

Forming and following conscience on this question cannot leave aside the elements already outlined at the level of the contents of a basic Christian conscience and in respect of the goods involved in marriage. Presupposing, for the sake of this argument, that a couple reach a judgment of conscience, at the level of intention, that they ought to avoid another pregnancy for the moment, this means that this is their honest assessment of God's will for them, a will they are obliged to follow in conscience. Turning to the question of the means to be used, direct abortion, direct sterilisation and contraception are excluded as morally legitimate ways of putting that intention into effect (n. 14). Natural family planning and therapeutic procedures with a contraceptive side-effect, where the conditions of double effect properly apply, do not violate these norms (nn. 15-16). How does 'follow your conscience' stand in regard to such norms?

The argument about infallibility was not just an academic one. For some writers it was seen as a pastoral question; if people knew that the doctrine had been taught infallibly, that the Magisterium could not have been wrong in teaching it, they would know that it was unquestionably true, that any doubts they might have had were false and should be set aside, and that they should implement the teaching in their marital lives. This

[24] Cf. ibid., nn. 64, 95.

consideration is certainly true and valid; that would be the implication of infallibility here.

If, on the other hand, it is judged in all honesty that infallibility is not at issue in this doctrine, then an *obsequium religiosum* is called for to the highest degree, since the least that can be said about the status of the doctrine is that the authoritative doctrine in the encyclical is certainly at the highest level of authoritative teaching.[25] The term *'obsequium'* certainly includes 'respect' for the Magisterium, but it means much more; it means to 'follow' the doctrine (*'sequi'*: to follow) or to 'submit' to it or to 'obey' it, not necessarily because the arguments for the teaching are persuasive, but for (*'ob'*: 'on account of') a religious motive (*'religiosum'*) that the teaching is given with the authority of Christ and in His Name and with the assistance of the Holy Spirit. This means that it has the presumption of truth and is unlikely to be wrong.

Some norms are given by the Second Vatican Council concerning conscience and Magisterium, in circumstances which imply a conflict or tension between conscience and a particular teaching. The Council states unambiguously that a person may not ignore a teaching of the Magisterium which has certainly been given and that they may not treat such a teaching as a mere opinion.[26] John Paul II takes this up in his allocution to moral theologians on the twentieth anniversary of *Humanae vitae* and thus with direct reference to the doctrine we are considering. No-one may consider that they are acting in good conscience if:

- they ignore the certain teaching of the Magisterium
- they treat that teaching as a mere opinion
- in doubt, they prefer their own opinion or that of

---

[25] Cf. *Lumen gentium*, n. 25.
[26] Cf. *Dignitatis humanae*, n. 14.

theologians to the certain teaching of the Magisterium.[27]

No Catholic could be acting in good conscience who chose just to ignore the doctrine of Paul VI's encyclical, nor who treated is as a mere opinion (not treating it as doctrine which ought to guide conscience). In his third point John Paul II goes beyond what was said in *Dignitatis humanae*, but on the basis of common moral theological doctrine. A person who has doubts about the doctrine of *Humanae vitae* ought to read the encyclical, if possible, and not just summaries of it or criticisms of it in the press. Such a person should try to understand it, embracing the key goods it proclaims and seeking to live by them, should try to accept it on the basis of theological arguments or for reasons of religious *obsequium*. He or she should seek advice from moral theologians or others who accept the teaching. However, as John Paul II notes, a person may remain in a state of real objective doubt as to the binding nature or truth of the doctrine. Anyone in a state of objective doubt has the obligation in conscience to act on the basis of the virtue of prudence, right reason in action. Part of the Catholic moral theological tradition has been the moral systems for resolving such doubts of conscience, at least to the extent of giving the person in doubt a subjective certitude that they would not be sinning by acting in a particular way. However, these moral systems presuppose that there is no Magisterial teaching on the precise matter of the person's doubt; it is for that reason that such a person would be advised to follow the well-argued (probable) opinion of approved theologians (those who accept Magisterial teaching and not those who deny it). In our encyclical, this is not the case at all; Paul VI certainly gave clear doctrine on contraception. It

---

[27] John Paul II, Allocution to the Second International Congress of Moral Theologians, 12 November, 1988, *L'Osservatore romano*, Italian edition, 17 November, 1988, 14-15.

is for this reason that John Paul II adds that, if in doubt, a person chose to follow their own personal opinion against Magisterial teaching on contraception, he or she could not be acting in good conscience. The same would be true if he or she, in such circumstances, chose to follow the opinions of theologians, even many of them, even famous ones, rather than follow the Magisterium's doctrine. In both instances, such a person would opt for mere opinion against what the Magisterium had certainly taught as morally normative. Rather, in doubt, a person should follow what the Magisterium has taught; anything else violates the virtue of prudence and is morally wrong.

c. Openness to Truth in Conscience and *Humanae vitae*

It should be sufficiently clear already that whatever 'follow your conscience' means, it does not mean doing as we please or making up our own version of what is morally right and wrong. When the Second Vatican Council spoke of human liberty or freedom as "an exceptional sign of the image of God in man", it added in the very same paragraph that such liberty was never to be confused with the 'licence' to do as we see fit.[28] Even if we were to be convinced, not through prejudice but in all honesty, that the doctrine contained in *Humanae vitae* were not infallibly proposed, 'follow your conscience' must mean to form our conscience on the basis of objective truth.

For Christians all moral matters must be looked at "in the light of revelation", in the light of Christ.[29] This does not mean having the arrogance to pretend to know 'what Christ would have done in this situation', particularly if it contrasts with teaching given in his Name and with the assistance of the Holy Spirit. Both the Council and Paul VI's encyclical give teaching on some fundamental goods,

---

[28] *Gaudium et spes*, n. 17.
[29] Ibid., nn. 33, 43.

which are not to be ignored by anyone seriously trying to reflect in conscience on responsible parenthood. They reflect what we might call the contents of a 'basic Christian conscience', goods which other people can and often do recognise and follow on the basis of their moral reason, or by natural moral law, but which are specifically and clearly rooted in Christian revelation. These include the fundamental good of marriage itself, as a community of life and love, involving fidelity, exclusivity, indissolubility, self-giving and receiving love of the couple and fecundity or fruitfulness. Love which does not include these particular goods is not truly marital love, but precisely in living by these goods in marriage couples can find their happiness and fulfilment. As tragic examples show, the violation of such key aspects of marriage and of conjugal love creates misery, bitterness and social fragmentation. Marriage does not succeed automatically, but requires mutual commitment at the wedding and also thereafter in the married life. The love which ought to unite the couple needs to be nurtured in all its dimensions and continually, since it will either grow and develop, or it will weaken. Christian spouses should deliberately reflect on their marriage as a basic good, on the various dimensions of that love in prayer and together in conversation on a regular basis. In such prayer and reflection they attend in conscience to what is truly good, to what ought to be sustained and promoted, to failings which need to be overcome, to God whom they encounter in conscience and who calls them to live this married life. Non-Christians too can reflect on these aspects of the good of marriage, to try to keep them in view and to live by them ever more fully and thereby to foster their own happiness as a couple and as a family.

Part of this reflection in conscience, and in the mutual exchanges of the couple, ought to involve a consideration of the requirements of responsible parenthood at the level of the couple's intentions (n. 10). It cannot be mere convenience nor selfish attitudes which lead to a judgment; it is a matter of what they ought to be seeking (a larger family or, for serious reasons, avoiding another pregnancy at present or indefinitely). A basic Christian conscience cannot regard procreation as an evil; it is a basic good for the human race as a whole and a basic good of marriage, implying also the upbringing of any children who may be born. The child cannot be thought of as an evil, a disease or an encumbrance to be disposed of, but only as a good, a gift from God, in whose coming to be they as spouses have a unique role in collaborating with His creative gift. Such an attitude to children needs to be fostered also in those who judge in sincerity of conscience that they themselves ought not to seek another child at the moment. Nor are most of these considerations just for Christians; they can be perceived by anyone open in conscience to the truth about the love and life which are at the heart of marriage. All married couples, forming their consciences and nurturing them in a continual and coherent way, must challenge the grave errors of those who deride marriage and the family, procreation and maternity, through prejudice or for reasons of an ideological nature.

4. Theological and Philosophical Arguments on Responsible Parenthood

One very important way to try to resolve a problem of conscience over this doctrine is to attend to what theologians who accept the teaching have said about it. They offer their opinions, but they may help explain at least some aspects of the question or may bring a different perspective to bear which may enable people in difficulties to rethink their position in conscience. Here it is intended to summarise some of the efforts which have been made to help people understand and follow the doctrine of *Humanae vitae*. They are not necessarily mutually exclusive.

a. Personalism, Natural Moral Law and Inseparability

Some presentations of natural moral law in recent centuries were very inadequate. Once the focus of reason, typical of Thomas Aquinas, was no longer central, there had been a tendency to think of it mainly as law, as willed by God, and to present it as such on the basis of the Church's Magisterium declaring something to be 'of natural law'. When the Enlightenment looked upon nature as no more than physical and biological realities, to be penetrated by reason, which they made an absolute and the sole criterion of truth, there was a tendency to respond to the claims being made in similar terms. This meant natural moral law was often presented in a reductive or partial way. Of course, biological realities are not irrelevant, especially in relation to responsible parenthood; they need to be understood and often need to be 'respected'. We ought not to interfere with the biological workings of our bodies unless there is a malfunction, a disability, a threat of illness or death resulting, if action is not taken. This is the basis of the principle of totality in its proper sense, justifying attempts to heal, prevent or limit the progress of illness.

In fact, it is not biological functioning itself which lies at the basis of natural law or of the doctrine on responsible parenthood. Rather, the latter means recognising the basic or fundamental human goods of love and of life which are involved. When moral reason functions correctly, marriage and conjugal love can be seen as basic goods to be respected by all and to be lived out by those with the vocation to marriage. So, too, the dimensions of those goods as presented by the Second Vatican Council and Paul VI can be seen as essential aspects of the good which they, as spouses, ought to promote and which they ought never directly to destroy. The same is true of the good of human life, including its transmission in procreation, again on the basis of the Conciliar and Papal teachings. This goes beyond mere biology and concerns truly human goods, fulfilling of human persons, especially of married couples. Directly and deliberately to violate such basic goods is intrinsically, morally wrong.

This was well put by an early defender of *Humanae vitae*: the principle of inseparability, that the unitive and procreative meanings of the conjugal act ought never deliberately to be separated from one another (n.12), is not making a statement about biology, but defends the truth that the couple's conjugal act transcends their love for one another, which it expresses, and is involved with the creative love of God as the source of new life, making every human being "the term of a personal love of God to which he *owes his identity*".[30] Such goods have to do with the very meanings of human existence and of marriage, meanings of a personalist character which go beyond biology, although we may not ignore such biological realities which condition the persons we are.[31] Respect for the place of God implies not violating the link between the meanings of the conjugal act as an act of unitive love between the couple and as being open, beyond that, to the unique collaboration with God as creator of new life in its procreative meaning. For Martelet, these two meanings

---

[30] G. Martelet, "Un profetismo contestato: il messaggio della Humanae vitae" in F. Guy, J. Zimmermann and D. Tettamanzi (a cura di), *Le coppie, l'amore, la vita* (Ancora, Milano, 1980), 253-271 at 258-259: emphasis in the original.

[31] Cf. idem, "Pour mieux comprendre l'encyclique 'Humanae vitae'", *Nouvelle revue théologique*, 90 (1968), I, 897-917 and II, "Signification et portée de l'encyclique", 1009-1063 at 911, 1029.

are joined together only in the fertile times of the wife's cycle, so that he sees the principle of inseparability, as a personalist and not just a biological reality, as applying only then.[32] A better interpretation is that which looks at these personalist realities as never to be directly attacked and as morally binding at all times; a couple whose intentionality is contraceptive reveals this at times by contracepting in the fertile periods and by using natural diagnostic methods in the infertile times, but that betrays a contraceptive intention throughout. On the other hand, a couple who respect both unitive and procreative meanings do so throughout the cycle, in their act of love they are open to the gift of new life from God, something to which a contracepting couple close themselves off.[33]

b. Contraception and a 'Contra-Life Will'

This approach to the difference between contraception and proper recourse to natural ways of diagnosing fertility and infertility claims that any couple, married or not, who contracept necessarily have a will which is opposed to life, a 'contra-life will'. It is not claimed that they actively recognise this to be the case or that they would even necessarily destroy new life through an abortion, although some would do that, but a couple who contracept choose to engage in an act which can give rise to new life and deliberately act to prevent it from doing so. They deliberately engage in an act which they consider might lead to conception (otherwise there is no reason to contracept), so that they envisage the possibility of a future child, and, through contraception, they act further to prevent that possible child from coming into existence.[34] This position is based on the earlier and long-

---

[32] Ibid., 1028.

[33] Cf. M. Séguin, "Nouveau point de vue sur la contraception", *Nouvelle revue théologique*, 112 (1990), 202-223 and 394-415 at 403-406.

[34] Cf. G. Grisez, J. Boyle, J. Finnis and W.E. May, "Every Marital Act Ought

standing condemnation of contraception in canon law as involving wrong-doing which was in some ways akin to homicide.[35] These authors, noting the real difference between contraception and homicide, see the similarity precisely in the couple having a contra-life will.

These authors distinguish having such a will from having emotional feelings against life.[36] Their argument provides an explanation for the immorality of all contraception, even outside of marriage. Nevertheless, the fact that many who contracept would never deliberately undertake an abortion were the contraception to fail and were the wife (or other woman) to become pregnant suggests that this is not the best way to understand the moral wrong of contraception. To say that their will is not contra-life to the same extent as in someone who would abort a child and yet that they still have a contra-life will such that any child conceived begins its life as unwanted, in essence is to say that they are inconsistent.[37] This subtle argument is not persuasive and, indeed, may make understanding the wrongfulness of contraception more difficult. Many who contracept, though, seem simply not to have a contra-life will, as their moral act of choosing against abortion demonstrates.

Treating contraception in a way akin to homicide was understandable in an age before the discovery in the early nineteenth century of how fertilisation or conception occurs because previously biology had judged that the sperm head contained a small human being ('homunculus') deposited in the vagina where he or she grew and developed. It seems correct to say that most

to be Open to New Life: Toward a Clearer Understanding", *The Thomist*, 52 (1988), 365-426 at 370-373.

[35] Ibid., 366, 374.
[36] Ibid., 375.
[37] Ibid., 386.

contracepting couples judge that they do not want or ought not to have a child at present, but that they act against their fertility, not against any existing person (as in homicide), in a way which seeks to prevent their sexual act from being fruitful.[38] On the other hand, couples engaging in sexual intercourse and using contraception, even for upright reasons of responsible parenthood, are not open to the gift of a child in the way they actually behave in contracepting.

The majority group on the Papal Commission before the encyclical and many supporters of contraception have drawn a sharp distinction between contraception and an 'anti-life mentality', condemning the latter, and between contraception and abortion.[39] What has often been underestimated is the extent to which contraception is not an isolated act, but is overwhelmingly a series of repeated acts, intentionally and in the actual conduct of the couple through what they positively do. They operate systematically against the procreative meaning of their conjugal acts to prevent or impede those acts from giving rise to new human beings. This cannot fail to increase the risk of children being seen as a problem, an obstacle or an object to be accepted or rejected only on their terms or at their convenience; in the end being reduced to 'objects of desire'. In this way, contraception is intrinsically contrary

---

[38] Cf. J.E. Smith, *Humanae Vitae: A Generation Later*, 361-366. Smith's distinction between 'prevent' and 'impede', however, used to contrast her position with that of Grisez, etc., is not convincing; they both translate accurately *'ut procreatio impediatur'* (n. 14) 'in such a way that procreation is prevented/impeded' and mean the same thing, as distinct from 'avoided'.

[39] See the observations in the 'majority report' of the Papal Commission prior to the encyclical, Documentum C ('Schema documenti de responsabili paternitate') in L. Rossi (a cura di), *Controllo delle nascite: il dossier di Roma* (Queriniana, Brescia, 1967), pars prima, II, n. 2, 180, approving of the condemnation of a selfish and contraceptive mentality in the totality of the conjugal life, and pars prima, IV, n. 2, 182, approving the condemnation of abortion.

to the 'good of the child' or to the *bonum prolis*' and increases the likelihood of children who are born being seen and treated as truly 'unwanted' and the risk of their subsequent care and upbringing being compromised; neglect and abuse of children in our time are certainly not automatically the result of contraception, but they are not unconnected with the mentality which contraception can foster. The more it is practised in a habitual way, the greater the risk too of a truly anti-life mentality developing and of abortion being seen and used as a form of contraception; here a 'contra-life will' is truly operative.[40] If contraception is not automatically 'contra-life' and if it is not as serious as abortion, it can too easily move in that direction from habitual practice. What we deliberately choose to do, our deliberate acts, especially in serious matters such as this, affect the way we think, the attitudes we develop and the persons we become. This Paul VI had appreciated when he had warned against the danger of married couples acting as if they were 'masters' of the sources of life rather than 'ministers' who respect them (n. 13) and when he had urged the need for living out the gift of human sexuality according to the virtue of chastity (nn. 10, 16 § 1, 21-22) .

c. Contraception, Inseparability and the Language of the Body

In line with the thinking of Martelet and Séguin, attention was focused on the 'language of the body'. This had been part of the 'personalism' which had been promoted often by those seeking a change in doctrine in their approach to natural moral law, which they had accused of being 'biologistic'. Correctly, they had stated that human beings

---

[40] This is apart from the fact that some forms of 'contraception' are, in fact, abortifacient, causing the destruction of the new human being, often by preventing his or her implantation in the endometrium (lining of the womb) by impairing its preparation to receive the new life conceived.

communicate through their body language, apart from through words, especially in the context of sexual love and of marriage. However, such approaches had often led to them regarding moral norms as 'ideals' not fully realisable where there might be a 'conflict of values' and where a greater good or lesser evil should be chosen for a grave reason (proportionalism), the kind of approach rejected by Paul VI as doing wrong to attain good (n. 14).[41] Despite their initial desire for 'personalism', they often ended up effectively identifying 'person' with 'reason', 'conscience' or 'spirit', treating the body and sexuality as somehow lesser realities. This violates the dignity of the human person, since the person is 'one in body and spirit', as we have seen, and since the body is part of who the human person is and not some object which he or she has at their disposal.[42]

Karol Wojtyla had already reflected on these questions as a philosopher. His analysis of sexual body language recognises the body as part of the person, the exteriority of the person, the essential and only way we have of communicating with one another as bodily human beings. Such communication we ought to exercise with full respect for one another as persons, never reducing the other person or ourselves to the level of an 'object' to be used for pleasure or some other purpose and then, in reality, to be discarded.[43] This is especially true of sexual encounters and especially of the intimate sexual language which is right only within marriage, as the community of enduring, faithful love, open to life, which enables

---

[41] Cf. John Paul II, *Veritatis splendor*, nn. 75-78.
[42] Cf. Second Vatican Council, *Gaudium et spes*, n. 14; Paul VI, *Humanae vitae*, n. 7 (and the Commentary above) and John Paul II, *Veritatis splendor*, nn. 48-50.
[43] Cf. K. Wojtyla, *Love and Responsibility*, revised edition, translated by H.T. Willetts (Ignatius, San Francisco, 1981), 37-40.

such sexual language to be expressed with full sincerity. The sexual differentiation of human beings as male and female and their basic complementarity make it possible to overcome the 'original' solitude of our first parent in the total, mutual gift of self with Eve when the two became 'one flesh' (Gen. 1:26-28, 2:5-24).[44] His recognition that our sexual passions have been disorientated by original sin and need to be redirected through the virtue of chastity to what is truly good and fulfilling for us as human beings recalls a truth about sexuality and marriage which had not been directly expressed in the Second Vatican Council (marriage as a remedy for concupiscence). This implies again the use of the most intimate sexual language only within marriage, but also that this language within marriage itself be directed only to what is good and be expressed in ways which are themselves good.

Precisely in relation to authentic sexual body language, John Paul II spoke of the two essential meanings of the conjugal act, the unitive and procreative meanings, and of the inseparable connection between them. The sexual body language of the conjugal act is only 'true' where these are both respected, as they are when that act is open to procreation and to union, while the language is contradictory, false and a 'lie' where these essential meanings are violated or contradicted, as they are in contraception. This is not only because they go against the procreative meaning of the act, since the couple are not open to new life in what they do when they contracept, but also because their apparently 'unitive' gesture is not truly unitive at all; instead of the unitive language

---

[44] Cf. John Paul II, Catechesis on Human Love, *The Theology of the Body: Human Love in the Divine Plan* (Pauline, Boston, 1997), cateches 9 (14 November, 1979), 10 (21 November, 1979), 14 (9 January, 1980), 45-51, 60-63: translation from *Uomo e donna lo creò: catechesi sull'amore umano* (Città Nuova, Roma, Libreria editrice Vaticana, Vatican, 1985).

of total self-giving and receiving, there is limited and conditional giving and receiving, on condition that their love not be fruitful in giving new life in conjunction with God.[45] This roots the explanation of the wrongfulness of contraception in specifically sexual behaviour, as distinct from acts against life.[46]

The recognition in conscience of the unity of the human being in his or her earthly existence, of being one in body and spirit, and especially of the moral good of the person as such which is to be respected in all we do implies not using ourselves or others as mere objects in our sexual or other behaviour, it means not treating the body as an object, but as part of the person, as sharing that personal dignity. The recognition of the goods of marriage (procreation and education, fidelity and indissolubility), of its ends (procreation and education, mutual help and remedying concupiscence) and of its essential meanings (unitive and procreative) as goods, ends and meanings to be respected and promoted by all of us is important. By promoting and defending them by what they say and do in general (e.g., in social exchanges, in politics), by not acting contrary to them, all Christians give witness to the Gospel in which they are rooted; Christian married couples give such witness more directly by living in accordance with them in their married lives. Yet, all people of goodwill can recognise these goods, ends and meanings when their moral reason functions correctly; they too can promote and defend them and non-Christian spouses, too, can express them more directly in their married lives.

This implies, however, that these goods, ends and meanings of marriage and of the conjugal act itself

---

[45] Cf. idem, Apostolic exhortation, *Familiaris consortio*, 22 November, 1981, n. 32.
[46] J.E. Smith, *Humanae Vitae: A Generation Later*, 360-361.

ought never to be directly and deliberately attacked, undermined or destroyed. This is so even if there are good reasons for trying to avoid another birth at present. An older natural law argument, the perverted faculty argument, was seen as implying that contraception was wrong because it interfered with the conjugal act itself. This was underestimating what was at issue, which is the moral good of procreation, of being open to a new human being, of being open to collaborating with God if he wishes to bestow such a gift and of being open to their own love blossoming in fruitfulness. To say the conjugal act has a procreative meaning does not mean that every such act will result in an actual procreation (we know this does not happen), but it means that it is the sort of act which could result in procreation, at least in principle, that it is a unique act of the spouses in that it is the only act they could perform themselves which could possibly result in the transmission of life, in collaboration with the creative act of God.[47] Even when there are good reasons to space births, if the spouses intervene actively to do something before, during or after the conjugal act (n. 14) to stop (prevent, impede) this from happening, they distort the whole meaning of this, their act. They do this not by violating some merely biological process, but by acting against its possible fruitfulness in the sense of attempting to prevent God granting them a new child even if it were his will to do so. In other words, they necessarily violate the procreative meaning, good or end, of their act. Since that act ought to be an act of their love, this means further that they are behaving in a contradictory way. Simultaneously they are thinking to

---

[47] Cf. M. Rhonheimer, "Contraception, Sexual Behavior and Natural Law – Philosophical Foundations of the Norm of 'Humanae vitae'" in A. Ansaldo (ed.), *Humanae vitae: 20 anni dopo: Atti del II congresso internazionale di teologia morale*, (Ares, Milano, 1989), 73-113 at 88-89, a slightly revised version of the original in *The Linacre Quarterly*, 56 (1989), 20-57.

express and deepen their love for one another in regard to the unitive meaning of their act, while deliberately acting to stop their love being fruitful. Yet, love of its very nature tends to blossom and grow, or it is weakening and failing; to act in this way through contraception is a contradiction of love itself. This is what John Paul II meant when he said that the couple's body language in contraception is a lie. That he went on to show that it is a lie also in respect of its unitive meaning, since it does not express true mutual self-giving, but restricts, conditions and contradicts it, confirms the importance also of the principle of inseparability.

In the case of periodic continence or the use of the natural cycle to avoid (but not prevent or impede) another birth at present, none of this happens. There the couple express their love fully through the conjugal act in the infertile period of the cycle, doing nothing to render their act unfruitful; their act is one of procreative meaning and reflects their intentionality throughout the cycle of doing nothing to violate this essential meaning of their acts. In the fertile period, they avoid the only way they could express love which might lead to a new life, in an act of procreative responsibility or respecting procreative meaning. There are other ways of being united in their love, of nurturing their love which are morally upright, which they can and should use especially in the fertile phase.[48]

d. Collaboration with the Creative Act of God

We have seen that individual acts are not to be underestimated, that they affect and reinforce our attitudes to moral goods and our patterns of behaviour and they affect the persons we are and become, the more so if they are of a serious or profound nature, such as is the conjugal

---

[48] Cf. M. Séguin, "Un nouveau point de vue sur la contraception", loc. cit., 219-222, 397-398.

act. This is true of the good we do and of the wrong we perpetrate. It is never enough to act from good intentions, although these are essential for acting in a morally upright way (hence, using 'natural methods' with contraceptive intent or as a means of contraception is morally wrong). What we deliberately choose to do to put into effect a good intention is also crucial to the moral uprightness of the act and of our behaviour. 'Weighing up' moral goods which are qualitatively different (e.g., justice and chastity, or marital fidelity and openness to new life) is impracticable and morally wrong. No basic human good ought ever to be directly and deliberately violated. Thus, the 'lesser evil' argument and the 'totality of the conjugal life' argument fail; a youth who steals to help out a widowed mother over a period of crisis cannot make that right by claiming to have lived justly at other times of his life.

Even a single act of contraception is wrong, since it violates the procreative good, end and meaning of marriage; it actually contradicts both its procreative and the unitive dimensions. What is specific about the conjugal act, apart from its being the most intimate and deeply personal way in which the spouses can unite themselves in love is that it is simultaneously the only act they could perform which can give rise to new life, in collaboration with God. Without God no new life can arise.[49] Those who do not know God or accept Him can still appreciate to some extent that new human life, the beginning of a new personal existence on earth, involves something which goes beyond them and beyond mere biology, although biological processes are necessary to its occurrence. This is not respected, but is violated, through contraception.

---

[49] Cf. M. Rhonheimer, *Natur als Grundlage der Moral: Die personale Struktur des Naturgesetzes bei Thomas von Aquin: Eine Auseinandersetzung mit autonomer und teleologischer Ethik* (Tyrolia, Innsbruck, Wien, 1987), 101-102 and footnote 10.

When reflecting upon conscience, we said that a couple's judgment, for upright reasons of responsible parenthood, at the level of intention, that they ought not to seek another child at present would be a sincere understanding of their moral duty and would represent their understanding of God's will for them. However, conscience is not infallible and can err, which means that a couple may be mistaken about God's will in regard to whether or not they should have another child at present. They should practise periodic continence, using whichever natural diagnostic technique suits them best to determine when the wife is in the fertile and when she is in the infertile time of the cycle and they should act accordingly, avoiding all contraception and behaving with full procreative responsibility at all stages of the cycle, as we have indicated. If they do this, then not only by their intention, but by what they deliberately do in practice, they are implementing their (perhaps mistaken) understanding of God's will and they are also truly and actually open to his will both in their intentions and in their actions. In other words, by not contracepting, should God choose to bestow upon them the gift of a child, they are open to God, to his gift, to new life. This is very different from the contracepting couple, even where they act from the same upright intention of avoiding another pregnancy because by what they do in contracepting their intercourse, they are not open to his will, to collaborating with his creative act, to his gift or to the new life he wishes to grant them.[50] Acting in harmony with human nature (n. 16) and the moral goods which fulfil them as persons and as spouses, spouses who do not contracept act not as if they were masters of the sources of life, neglectful of God's role and of his will, but as ministers of his plan (n.

---

[50] Cf. M. Séguin, loc. cit., 408-413.

13), to which they are open both in intention and in the way they deliberately choose to behave, and they give a coherent witness to the goods of marriage. They show also the proper disposition of conscience, to be open to the truth and to God always, ready in intention and in practice to adapt themselves to him and to his will.

5. *Humanae vitae* and later developments

Very briefly, it is intended to make some observations about three issues which have emerged since 1968 to which the doctrine of *Humanae vitae* does apply or might apply.

a. Assisted and Substitutive Procreation

The question of conjugal sterility had been addressed by Pius XII and, indeed, his teachings have provided the core elements of subsequent doctrine. However, the practical implementation of *in vitro* fertilisation (in a glass) in the late 1970s raised the matter in a more dramatic form. The Congregation for the Doctrine of the Faith used the principle of inseparability which we have seen to have been a development of doctrine in *Humanae vitae* and to have played an important role in grounding and illuminating the doctrine on contraception, but this time in the reverse sense, in a way which Paul VI would not have envisaged. If any form of artificial insemination involving third-party donors of gametes (sperm or ova) was to be rejected as a violation of marriage and as akin to adultery, the question was raised about the possibility of artificial insemination by husband, as under Pius XII, and about *in vitro* fertilisation, using gametes only from husband and wife. If the wrong of masturbation for the collection of sperm were avoided and if the malice of abortion, stemming from the deliberate creation of multiple embryos, resulting from the stimulation of the ovaries to produce several ova, were also to be avoided, then might not married couples with a problem of sterility make use of these new technologies? Even in this so-called 'simple case' of *in vitro* fertilisation, the Congregation responded negatively, since such fertilisation would entail separating the procreation of the child from the couple's conjugal act, violating the principle of inseparability in the opposite way from contraception.[51] In effect, the gametes would have to be collected from the couple, even after a conjugal act with the seminal fluid being aspirated, but the wife would be under anaesthetic when it came to transferring the embryo. As tragic cases of couples having a child of whom neither is a parent or of whom one is not the parent have illustrated, it is really third-party technicians (here mixing up gametes or embryos) who bring the sperm and ova into contact and not the couple. Such technicians do this in a laboratory and the transfer of the embryo is not the personal act of the couple. Fertility clinics often require 'clients' to sign forms, permitting an abortion if a handicap is suspected, so that the compromise with abortion, even in the 'simple case', is not easily avoided.

Ways of assisting sterile couples include work on prevention of sterility, which should include avoiding long-term contraception, chemical or mechanical, which often distorts or damages the woman to the point where she cannot or cannot easily have children, when she wants them. Various procedures can be undertaken to cure some types of sterility, where there is a careful diagnosis of its precise nature or to circumvent other obstacles to procreation. Here, too, though, it is important for the love of the couple to be nurtured, to avoid what in some cases can be an obsessive preoccupation with having a child to the exclusion of much else, even of the other spouse.

---

[51] Cf. Congregation for the Doctrine of the Faith, Instruction on Respect for Human Life in its Origins and on the Dignity of Procreation, *Donum vitae*, 22 February, 1987, II, B, 4, a, and 5.

b. The Condom and HIV

The HIV and even AIDS is not an infection, but is a contagion, contractable through physical contact of body fluids and so also by sexual transmission. Where a married couple has one spouse HIV positive, it is suggested by some that a condom may be used to prevent the transmission of the virus to the healthy spouse. For the purposes of this discussion, it does not affect matters whether the spouse with the contagion contracted it innocently (e.g., from a blood transfusion where sufficient care was not taken to test the blood properly or other such instances) or through immoral behaviour.

Various arguments have been proposed to try to justify the use of the condom here.

i. Double Effect

A married couple has the right (and normally the duty) to express their love for one another also sexually. Using a condom might be said to have two effects, one of avoiding the transmission of the virus (good) and one contraceptive (bad), that the intention would be directed towards the first, with the second being outside or beyond the intention, that the good effect would not be attained through the contraception, and that there would be a proportionate reason of expressing love as a couple.

Apart from whether or not the uncontaminated spouse might be put, or feel, under pressure to accept what in reality he or she would not want, this argument fails because there is another and better method of preventing the contagion spreading, namely abstinence, since the duty to engage in sex is not absolute and does not apply in this case. Secondly, it is not clear that the contraceptive effect is completely beyond the intention, nor that the good effect is not attained at least in part through it, since the couple would wish to avoid transmitting the virus to any child who might be conceived. Thus, contraception would be also part of the intention either expressly or effectively and would also be the very means by which any transmission to a child would be avoided. Thirdly, conjugal intercourse ought to express love, but a spouse with a potentially lethal contagion ought to do all that is possible to avoid it spreading to the one person he or she ought to love more than anyone else on earth.[52]

ii. Legitimate Self-Defence

Where public authority, responsible for safety and observance of the law, is not available or is unable to intervene effectively and where a person or persons are actually or imminently victims of an unjust aggression, it is allowed to use reasonable force to repel the aggressor, even if he dies as a result. The claim is made that the HIV virus is the 'unjust aggressor' and the condom a means of legitimate self-defence.

It is certainly true that it is legitimate and even obligatory to try to protect our health against what threatens it. However, the term 'unjust aggressor' is used here in an analogous sense. The virus does not spread, as might an infection, through air particles, but by some exposure to lesions by touching where it enters the body of another. The point here is that, in sexual intercourse between the spouses, it is the spouses who initiate the intercourse or who facilitate any 'aggression' in and through what is presented as an act of love. There is not true aggression here at all. Rather, it is a spouse who deliberately exposes his or her married partner to a lethal disease, something they ought not to do.

---

[52] Cf. G.J. Woodall, "The use of the Condom to Prevent the Transmission of H.I.V.", *Medicina e morale* (1998), 545-579 at 551-552, 567-569.

The argument from *Humanae vitae* that it is legitimate to use therapeutic measures to cure a disease of the organism, even if a contraceptive effect is foreseen (n. 15), implies the use of double effect and implies perhaps also the argument about unjust aggression. Apart from the dangers of the condom splitting or not being properly employed, which are not negligible, a proportionate reason under double effect entails that no other means be available of attaining the good effect without engaging the bad effect, but abstinence is exactly such an alternative and better means.[53]

c. Rape and other violent sexual intercourse

Where an army is marauding in an area and where it is known that soldiers are quite systematically raping women, it is legitimate, in principle, to use a contraceptive which is not abortifacient as a means of legitimate self-defence. Here the conditions of double effect would apply. This would be a case of foreseen rape.

Where rape has actually occurred, the sperm are to be seen as the extension of the unjust aggression. If ovulation has not occurred, a contraceptive pill which is not abortifacient is likely to impede conception. In reality, differing combinations of synthesised oestrogen and progesterone are found in 'the pill' (often with lower oestrogen levels to seek to avoid damaging side-effects to the woman's health from long-term use). They function in single, double or triple phased action, but the properly contraceptive effect of blocking ovulation is more likely to operate if taken in the days immediately preceding ovulation. The 'back-up' action of these pills is abortifacient, preventing implantation of the newly conceived human being. In the case of the 'morning after pill', massive doses of oestrogen and of progesterone are

---

[53] Cf. ibid., 550-551, 566-567.

used; it is taken at two points, 12 hours apart, the first can be over 60% effective as a contraceptive but thereafter has a 'back-up' abortifacient action, the second being clearly abortifacient in its action.[54] If it were restricted to the first administration, but *only after a test had shown that ovulation had not yet occurred*, it could perhaps be legitimate after rape, since the verification that ovulation had definitely not occurred, followed immediately by taking this high dosage pill would mean that it would act almost certainly as a true contraceptive. However, to undertake tests to see whether or not ovulation has taken place and to await results is not likely to be welcomed. Since conception can occur within 24 hours or up to three days (since the sperm can survive that long), there is little time to check. It is, of course, entirely legitimate for the woman concerned to have a vaginal 'wash out' after the rape, to remove the sperm, the extension of the aggression.

What makes the difference once conception has occurred is the presence of a new human being, entirely innocent of all wrong-doing and in no sense at all an aggressor or the mere extension of an aggression. As with every newly conceived human being, he or she is to be respected and treated as a person from the first moment of conception, from the formation of the zygote, whose basic human rights are to be respected, among which is the fundamental right of all innocent human beings to life.[55] Hence any pill or other procedure used to remove or destroy the newly conceived child is a directly procured abortion, always gravely immoral, whatever the intention.

---

[54] Cf. M-L. Di Pietro and R. Minacori, "Sull'aboritività della pillola estrogenica e di altri 'contracettivi' ", *Medicina e morale* (1996), 863-900 at 868-869, 878-880 and 890-892; E. Sgreccia, *Manuale di bioetica*, I, *Fondamenti ed etica biomedica* (Vita e pensiero, Milano, 2007), 515-517.

[55] Cf. *Donum vitae*, n. I, 1.

The difficulty in both of these cases is the fact that, nowadays, the lower oestrogen pill, with a higher level of progesterone, is what is mostly available. Its main action is as an abortifacient, as would be prostaglandin, the RU486 pill, an IUD coil. Recent ideologically inspired changes in terminology (inventing the term 'pre-embryo' prior to 14 days or now simply not referring to an embryo until after 14 days, as well as re-defining conception as successful implantation) are designed to facilitate destructive research on embryos prior to implantation and to re-label as merely contraceptive pills and devices which in truth are abortifacient. Given the fact that most pills on the market operate mainly as abortifacients at least in their 'back up', practically, it is not a morally licit option to employ them, even after rape. A vaginal 'wash out' is licit.

The case of violent sexual intercourse between husband and wife (at times called rape within marriage) in my view could require or legitimate following the norms just outlined. The argument that foreseen rape in general could be susceptible to self-defence, using a contraceptive but not abortifacient pill, has been said to rest upon such sexual intercourse not having been the object of free consent. It is then stated that, on the contrary, married couples have consented to all acts of intercourse throughout the course of their married lives and that the acts are part of 'freely consented intercourse', not legitimating self-defence.[56] This claim is to be questioned. It is highly doubtful that a wife would have consented to sexual acts imposed upon her with violence or with the threat of violence. If, for the sake of argument, she had consented also to such acts, her consent to those acts precisely as such would be invalid. (This is not to say that the marital consent as such is

---

[56] Cf. M. Rhonheimer, "Contraception, Sexual Behavior and Natural Law", loc. cit., 86.

invalid, although it might be.) This is because such acts are immoral and any contract which has as its object an immoral act or collaborating in an immoral act, is itself morally invalid. In fact, there would be no duty to fulfil such a promise, even if it had been made under oath; rather, there would be a duty not to perform such an act, since it would be immoral.

Apart from the practical difficulty of finding contraceptive but not abortifacient pills, it has to be said that self-defence used in this way in marriage would be unlikely to work, where the abuse were constant or repeated. Its use, if known to the husband, might encourage him to act in this way all the more because he would worry less about a possible pregnancy. A woman facing such repeated danger needs help from the authorities; a legal separation might be necessary.

6. Conclusion

The encyclical *Humanae vitae* was not only the most controversial of the last century, but was one of the most important. Its rich message is full of hope for spouses, is rooted in an understanding of the goods of marriage and of authentic conjugal love, in full harmony with the Second Vatican Council. Its teaching on responsible parenthood is not simple, but it is immensely valuable. It is hoped that this commentary may have helped to dispel some misunderstandings of Paul VI's encyclical and that it may have helped people to appreciate some of its depths of meaning, especially that married couples may find its teaching more accessible and may be encouraged to live in accordance with the truth which it proclaims in such a prophetic manner.

SELECT BIBLIOGRAPHY

Second Vatican Council, *Gaudium et spes*, Pastoral Constitution on the Church in the Modern World, nn. 47-52 and 87 (C.T.S., London)

John Paul II, *Familiaris consortio*, Apostolic exhortation, 1981 (C.T.S., London)

John Paul II, *Man and Woman He Created them: A Theology of the Body*, new edition of the Papal catecheses on human love given between 1979 and 1984 (Pauline, Boston, Mass., 2006)

Anscombe, G.E.M., *Contraception and Chastity* (C.T.S., London)

Cappella, A., *The Natural Way: The Billings Method: A Simple and Reliable Method of Fertility Regulation* (BBE, Torino, 1985)

Cessario, R., *The Virtues or the Examined Life* (Continuum, London, 2002)

Estevez, J.M., *"Male and Female He Created Them": On Marriage and the Family* (Ignatius, San Francisco, 2003)

Ford, J.C., and G. Grisez, "Contraception and the Infallibility of the Ordinary Magisterium", *Theological Studies*, 39 (1978), 258-312.

Grabowski, J.S., *Sex and Virtue: An Introduction to Sexual Ethics* (Catholic University of America Press, Washington, D.C., 2003)

Grisez, G., *Contraception and the Natural Law* (Bruce, Milwaukee, 1964)

Grisez, G., *The Way of the Lord Jesus*, II, *Living a Christian Life* (Herald Press, Quincy, Illin., 1993)

Grisez, G., J. Boyle, J. Finnis and W.E. May, "Every Marital Act Ought to Be Open to Life: Toward a Clearer Understanding", *The Thomist* 52 (1988), 365-426.

von Hildebrand, D., *Humanae Vitae: A Sign of Contradiction* (Franciscan Herald Press, Chicago, 1969)

Hilgers, T., *The Creighton Model NaProEducation System*, 3rd edition (Pope Paul VI Institute Press, Omaha, Neb., 1996)

Kippley, J. and S., *The Art of Natural Family Planning* (Couple to Couple League, Ohio, 1982)

Lawler, R., J. Boyle and W.E. May, *Catholic Sexual Ethics: A Summary, Explanation and Defense* (Our Sunday Visitor, Huntington, Ind., 1998)

May, W.E., *Sex, Chastity and Marriage: Reflections of a Catholic Layman, Spouse and Parent* (Franciscan Herald Press, Chicago, 1981)

Shivanandan, M., *Natural Sex* (Hamlyn, Feltham, 1979)

Shivanandan, M., *Crossing the Threshold of Love: A New Vision of Marriage in the Light of John Paul II's Anthropology* (Catholic University of America Press, Washington, D.C., 1999)

Smith, J.E., *Humanae Vitae: A Generation Later* (Catholic University of America Press, Washington, D.C., 1991)

Smith, J.E., *Why Humanae Vitae was Right: A Reader* (Ignatius, San Francisco, 1993)

West, C., *Theology of the Body Explained: A Commentary on John Paul II's 'Man and Woman He Created Them'*, revised edition (Pauline, Boston, Mass., 2007)

Wojtyla, K., *Love and Responsibility* (Ignatius, San Francisco, 1991)

Wojtyla, K., *Fruitful and Responsible Love* (St. Paul's, Slough, 1978)

Zimmerman, A., F. Guy and D. Tettamanzi, *Natural Family Planning, Nature's Way – God's Way* (St. Cloud, Minnesota, 1980)